Green Economics

Second edition

—

David Burningham
Brunel University
and
John Davies
Coleg Harlech, Gwynedd

Series Editor
Susan Grant
West Oxfordshire College

Heinemann Educational Publishers
Halley Court, Jordan Hill, Oxford OX2 8EJ
a division of Reed Educational & Professional Publishing Ltd

OXFORD   MELBOURNE   AUCKLAND
JOHANNESBURG   BLANTYRE   GABORONE
IBADAN   PORTSMOUTH (NH) USA   CHICAGO

Heinemann is a registered trademark of Reed Educational & Professional
Publishing Ltd

© David Burningham and John Davies, 1995, 1999

First published in 1995 in the Studies in the UK Economy series

Second edition published 1999

03 02 01 00 99
10 9 8 7 6 5 4 3 2 1

British Library Cataloguing in Publication Data

A catalogue record for this book is available from the British Library

ISBN 0 435 33210 4

Typeset and illustrated by TechType, Abingdon, Oxon.

Printed and bound in Great Britain by Biddles Ltd, Guildford

Acknowledgements

The publishers would like to thank the following for permission to reproduce copyright
material:

The Associated Examining Board for the questions on pp. 57, 81; The CBI for the material
on p. 37; The *Daily Post* for the extracts on p. 64 and 77; DETR for the material on p. 37;
The Economist for the articles on pp. 11, 56, 100, 118, © The Economist, London
(11/7/98, 22/8/98, 18/4/98, 18/9/93); Edexcel Foundation for the questions on pp. 36,
118–19; *Financial Times* for the article on p. 25; *The Guardian* for the articles on pp. 4,
67, 75; HMSO for the material on pp. 17, 38, 67, 71, 78, 109: Crown copyright is
reproduced with the permission of the Controller of Her Majesty's Stationery Office; *The
Independent* for the articles on pp. 99, 107; *New Scientist* for the extract on p. 68; News
International Syndication for the article on pp. 13–14, © Times Newspapers Limited,
1999; OCR for the questions on pp. 27, 50–1, 58–60, 80–81, 92–4, 102–5, 118; Pluto
Press for the extract from *The Green Economy*, by Michael Jacobs (Pluto Press, 1991), on
p. 76; *Punch* for the cartoons on pp. 45, 54, reproduced by permission of Punch Ltd;
Bryan Reading for the cartoon on p. 111, published and reproduced by permission of *The
Oldie*; Steer Davies Gleave for the material on p. 36; The Telegraph for the extracts on pp.
50, 103; The Yorkshire Evening Post for the article on p. 27.

The publishers have made every effort to contact copyright holders. However, if any
material has been incorrectly acknowledged, the publishers would be pleased to correct
this at the earliest opportunity.

Contents

iii

Preface

The *environment* figures prominently in the new A level Economics specifications and in most economic and business studies courses. It is easy to see why. Environmental issues are being discussed from the local to the world level. Environmental economics is also an area that enables students to develop and apply economic concepts and skills to tackle real and important problems.

The first edition of *Green Economics* provided readers with a clear, up-to-date and insightful coverage of the key aspects of environmental economics. In this new edition, the authors build on that work by exploring, in more depth, a range of issues including waste disposal legislation and, in particular, *cost–benefit analysis* (CBA). A new chapter has been devoted to the technique of cost–benefit analysis. This explains in a reader-friendly manner the stages of CBA.

Throughout the book, points are well illustrated by reference to real-life environmental issues and the British government's and world response to those issues.

Sue Grant
Series Editor

Introduction

'People everywhere are offended by pollution. They sense intuitively that we have pressed on limits we should not have exceeded. They want to clean up the World, make it a better place, be good trustees of the Earth for future generations.'
James Speth, President of the World Resource Institute

This book is about the contribution economics can make to the solution of environmental problems. We intend to show that, although the challenges referred to by James Speth in the quotation above are tasks for, among others, scientists and conservationists, they also raise questions about choice and efficiency in the use of limited resources. They are therefore part of the study of economics.

- **Chapter 1** reviews the questions economists ask about the environment.

- **Chapter 2** examines the economic causes of environmental problems.

- **Chapter 3** continues with those themes and discusses what is meant by 'efficient' pollution.

- **Chapter 4** explores the relationships between growth and environmental damage.

- **Chapter 5** looks at the question of how we measure the value of environmental benefits and the costs of environmental damage.

- **Chapter 6** shows how we can use these calculations of costs and benefits for the particular projects, to decide on the amount of resources needed to save and improve the environment.

- **Chapters 7, 8 and 9** discuss the measures that can be taken to improve the management of environmental resources, from both theoretical and practical standpoints, with reference to UK and European experience.

Chapter One

The environment and the economy

'I shot an arrow in the air. It stuck!'
Tom Lehrer, songwriter and mathematician

Preliminaries

The plight of the world environment may provoke solemn statements, or wry jokes of the kind quoted above. Whatever our response, the environment is clearly a matter of widespread anxiety and fascination, guaranteed a prominent place in television and newspaper headlines.

The boxed news item 'Nuclear waste' typifies our changing attitude to the environment. In the past, environmental activists were usually seen as irritating and dangerous eccentrics. Now the very targets of their protests are acknowledged by governments and business corporations worldwide.

NUCLEAR WASTE

● *Boarding of nuclear waste ship by protesters*

A ship carrying nuclear waste through the Panama Canal on behalf of British Nuclear Fuels was boarded on 6 February 1998 by three activists from the environmental group Greenpeace. The three chained themselves to the ship's mast but were removed after some three hours. The vessel, which had set sail from France, was carrying the third and, to date, the largest nuclear waste cargo from Europe to Japan.

● *Talks on hazardous waste export ban*

Representatives of more than 100 governments and the European Commission began talks on 23 February 1998 in Kuching, Malaysia, on the establishment of a worldwide export ban on hazardous waste, in order to protect developing countries.

Source: *Keesing's News Digest 1998*

Major disasters in the 1980s and 1990s, such as:

- the massive radiation leak from the Ukrainian nuclear plant at Chernobyl
- the 11 million gallon oil spill from the Exxon tanker *Valdez*, destroying 1300 miles of Alaskan fisheries and coastal wildlife
- the devastating explosion, killing 6600 people, at a chemical plant in Bophal, India
- the poisonous smog from man made forest fires in Malaysia and Indonesia, spreading over 2000 miles and reaching 70 million people
- tens of thousands of tonnes of toxic metals deposited near Europe's largest nature reserve in Spain after a dam had collapsed

have helped to focus attention on the serious environmental impact of human activities.

In the United Kingdom, the efforts of Greenpeace, Friends of the Earth and the Green party have ensured that the environment is firmly on the political agenda. The publication in 1990 of *This Common Inheritance* – the first official survey of all aspects of the UK environment – signalled the government's involvement. It is significant that six of the thirteen so-called 'quality-of-life indicators' now published annually by the government (see the box on the next page) are directly related to the environment. Today all political parties claim to be 'green', as do most large corporations.

Since one country's pollution can be every country's problem, let us look for a moment at the environment from a global perspective. According to a much publicized United Nations report, glaciers are shrinking, sea levels rising and the planet is warming (Figure 1).

The gloomy statistics of this report also portray a world in which natural stocks and resources are dwindling as demand increases. If the trends continue, it is claimed that dependable supplies of ocean and freshwater fish, and of fertile land, may be depleted within two generations.

How seriously should we regard these forecasts and what have they to do with economics? This book explores two questions:

- To what extent are environmental problems also economic problems?
- From our toolkit of economic ideas and techniques, are there any that we can use to help us repair or check the damage to our planet?

THIRTEEN QUALITY-OF-LIFE INDICATORS

Economic growth	Total output of the economy. Standard measure is gross domestic product (GDP). Since 1970, output has increased by 80 per cent in real terms
Social investment	Measures investment in 'public assets' such as railways, buses, roads, hospitals, schools, water and sewerage. Accounts for 10 per cent of all capital spending and about 2 per cent of GDP.
Employment	Income enables individuals to improve their living standards. Since 1994, employment rate has increased slowly to current 73 per cent.
Health	Average life expectancy is now around 74 years for men and 79 for women, but the time people can expect to live in good health is some years less.
Education and training	Based on qualifications at age 19.
Housing quality	Measures numbers of homes unfit to live in. In 1996, the private rented sector had the highest proportion of unfit stock – 15.1 per cent.
Climate change	Based on greenhouse gas emissions. UK emissions of the 'basket' of greenhouse gases fell by 5 per cent between 1990 and 1996.
Air pollution	In urban areas, the average number of days when pollution was recorded as moderate or worse fell from 62 days in 1993 to 40 in 1997.
Transport	Motor vehicle traffic in 1997 was more than eight times the level in 1950, and car traffic was over 14 times higher.
Water quality	According to number of rivers of good or fair quality – currently nearly 95 per cent of UK river networks.
Wildlife	Based on population of wild birds – regarded as a good indicator of wildlife and the health of the wider environment. Populations of farmland and woodland birds have been in decline since the mid-70s.
Land use	New homes built on previously developed land. In England, about 55 per cent of homes are built on brownfield sites, against a government target of 60 per cent by 2008.
Waste	An estimated 145 million tonnes of waste are produced in the UK each year, of which over 60 per cent are disposed of in landfill sites.

Source: *The Guardian*, 24 November 1998

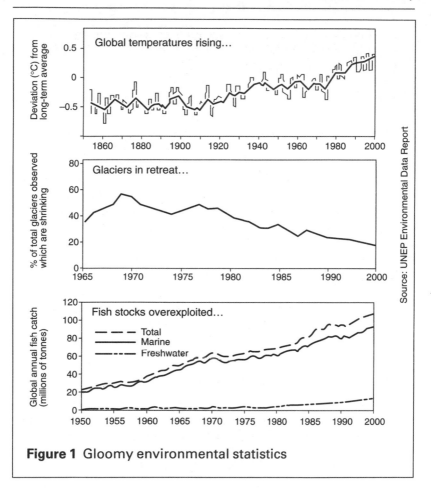

Figure 1 Gloomy environmental statistics

Before tackling these questions we need to be clear about the nature of the major threats to the earth's environment. These have been a source of considerable confusion in the public mind, for several reasons:

- Eco-systems – the relationships between living things and their surroundings – are very complex. Scientists are not yet in agreement about the significance of some of the environmental threats or ways in which they occur.
- The complicated physics and chemistry of climate are also equally difficult for scientists to understand. Good and bad effects may coexist. Recent research, for example, has shown that sulphur dioxide gas, released when coal and oil are burnt, creates a protective haze that reflects some sunlight back into space, thereby

slowing the harmful global warming effect arising from human activities. Unfortunately for us, sulphur dioxide also contributes to acid rain, damaging lakes and forests.

• Further confusion can arise in the mind of the keen citizen with an interest in the environment, because some desirable green activities may have undesirable side-effects. The loyal, green-car owner, having fitted a catalytic converter to reduce exhaust emissions, may be dismayed to hear experts pronounce that the benefits are offset by higher fuel consumption. Some green pressure groups themselves are partly responsible for confusion over the extent of environmental damage. In an effort to promote their cause, they may offer a doomsday scenario which plays down progress in managing the environment – the reduction in the use of harmful chemicals such as CFCs, for example.

• Doom-laden forecasts, if proved wrong, may misfire, by reducing interest in things that should be matters of serious concern. In 1968, two influential studies, *Limits of Growth* and *Mankind at the Turning Point,* predicted, on the basis of a computer model of the world, widespread catastrophe and international collapse of economies within two decades, as natural resources were exhausted. The world demand for petroleum was forecast to exceed supply by 1990. *The computer model failed to incorporate the elementary economic lesson that scarcity drives up prices and prompts a search for new reserves and alternatives.* Nevertheless, over twenty years later, population growth – the basis of these forecasts – is still a real and persistent problem.

• Fashion and sentimentality also add to our misunderstanding about environmental problems. Politicians, media stars and various pressure groups gain useful publicity by their visible support of popular 'green' concerns. Public attention and funds are then focused on the necessity of saving spectacular whales or cuddly giant pandas. The disappearance of less attractive species, such as the Central American Harlequin Beetle or Brazilian Pit Viper – whose venom is useful to our understanding of the treatment of high blood pressure – go unnoticed.

Environmental threats

To help give some perspective on what is sometimes a rather confusing picture, Table 1 lists some estimates of the major threats to the environment. No attempt has been made to put them in order of importance or comment on the accuracy of the estimates. That is still a matter of fierce argument.

Table 1 Environmental threats

Over-population
- Now estimated at 6 billion, up 3 billion from 1960, it is increasing by nearly 90 million every year (equivalent to the combined populations of the UK, Ireland, the Benelux countries and Denmark).
- Estimated to stabilize at between 11 and 15 billion by 2200, this is more than the planet can adequately support.
- 90 per cent of the growth is concentrated in countries least able to sustain it.
- It is estimated that half the world's population will within two decades be living in mega-cities – with substantial slums and squatter settlements in developing countries.

Species extinction
- Destruction of forests and other habitats is driving an estimated 100 species of plants and animals to extinction every week.
- The losses are particularly serious in the tropical forests, which cover only 7 per cent of the earth's surface but are a home to between 50 and 80 per cent of the planet's species.
- Genetic material being lost may contain means of fighting diseases or improving crops.
- In the UK each year about 1 per cent of the 5600 Sites of Special Scientific Interest suffer damage which may be irreversible.

Destruction of the resource base
Depletion of finite, non-renewable resources is still a matter of concern but attention is now on the threat to renewable resources:
- Deforestation – tropical forests shrink annually by an estimated 80 000 square miles (1 per cent) each year.
- This probably intensifies the greenhouse effect because tropical rainforests take in carbon dioxide and give out oxygen.
- Fisheries depletion – most experts are agreed that the limit to sustainable landing of wild fish has been exceeded. In more and more waters, too few fish have been left to maintain stocks.
- About 17 per cent of the world's soil is now considered degraded by overgrazing, unsustainable irrigation and other types of poor land management.

Waste
- The UK produces more than 145 million tons of industrial and household waste a year. Over 60 per cent goes in landfill. More than two million tons are dumped in the sea.
- As nations produce more waste, the world is running out of places to dispose of refuse safely.
- Organic wastes and fertilizers in high concentrations can affect water supplies and cause serious health hazards. Persistent toxic wastes – pesticides, lead, mercury, etc. – become ingested by animals and plants. They may remain in the food chain, eventually reaching a dangerous level on a worldwide scale.

Air pollution
- Local air pollution – smoke, carbon-monoxide from car exhausts and nitrogen oxide from industry – if concentrated, can cause lung and respiratory illnesses.
- Worldwide air pollution – industrial emissions, sulphur oxides and nitrogen oxides – react with water vapour to create acid rain, which is harmful to buildings, plants and animal life. At least 22 Scottish lochs are acidified.
- CFC (chloro-fluro-carbon) gases contribute to the depletion of the ozone layer which protects the air from injurious ultraviolet radiation. A 1 per cent decrease in the earth's ozone layer can cause a 3 per cent increase in skin cancer and a 1 per cent fall in the yield of certain crops. It is calculated that over Europe a 10 per cent reduction has occurred in the ozone layer in the past 10 years.

Global warming
- Carbon-monoxide and other 'greenhouse gases' contribute to the trapping of heat between the earth's surface and the atmosphere. Consequent higher sea levels may produce damaging climatic changes.

It will be noticed that they are not all related to pollution. The extinction of species, for example, is just as much due to the disruption of habitats – housing and road building in industrial countries, and deforestation in developing countries – as it is to poisonous wastes and herbicides.

The environment and opportunity cost

What has this varied group of problems got to do with economics? It will be argued, quite rightly, that they raise political, moral and social questions, as well as matters of scientific debate. Nevertheless, they all have one thing in common – **scarcity**. This is what economics is about – the arrangements that societies make for the use and development of their scarce resources. Environmental problems would not arise if there was a superabundance of resources. There would be no worries about running out of supplies. Most waste products could be easily and harmlessly dispersed if there were boundless oceans and atmosphere. Many of our environmental problems occur simply because we have tended to treat world resources as if they were limitless.

Scarcity forces upon us the necessity of making choices by comparing alternatives. If limited resources are fully employed, an increase in the output of one commodity or service can only be achieved by having less of another – more resources used to clean up the environment means fewer resources available for consumer goods.

This is shown in a simplified form in Figure 2 (a). This curve shows, with given productive resources and technology, the choices facing a society. The vertical axis measures the amount of consumer goods produced, while the horizontal axis measures the alternative effects of using resources to raise environmental standards. This could be measured by an **index of environmental quality** including such things as air and water purity, toxic waste disposal and noise levels.

The curve shows the different combinations of consumer goods and environmental standards available. If all resources are used for consumer goods, C_0 will be produced with zero environmental quality. Alternatively, if all resources were devoted instead to the environment, with no consumer goods, environmental quality would be at a level of E_0. Along the **production possibility curve** (PPC), there are various combinations of consumer goods and environmental quality. In practice it is unlikely that any community would reduce its environmental standards to zero – some minimum amount of waste disposal, for example, would be essential. Equally, no society, however 'green', will use all of its resources to raise environmental standards. The practical choices are indicated by the proportion of the curve contained in the dotted quadrant.

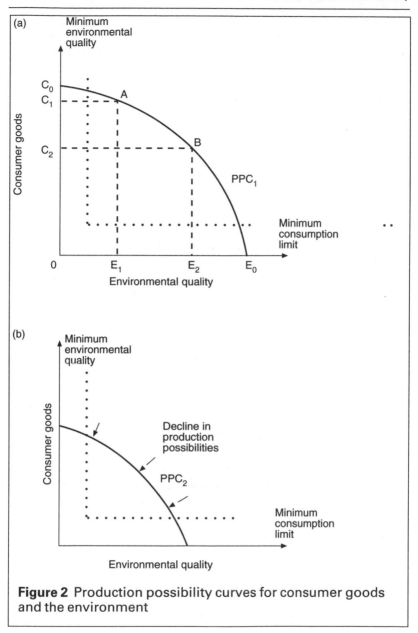

Figure 2 Production possibility curves for consumer goods and the environment

Assume that a society is at A on the PPC. The level of output is C_1 and environmental standards are E_1, and it is desired to raise standards to E_2. – or shift from A to B on the PPC, curve. This involves the transfer of resources to environmental use and reduction of consumer goods output to C_2. This assumes, of course, that resources are fully employed and used efficiently. The **trade-off**, the increase from E_1 to E_2 in exchange for a reduction of consumer goods output from C_1 to C_2, is known as the **opportunity cost** of the increase in environmental standards.

Here it must be emphasized that decisions today about the amount of resources used for environmental standards may have an impact on the production possibilities for future generations.

Consider again point A, with a high output of consumer goods C_1 and very low output of environmental quality E_1. In the long run this may reduce the production possibility curve to a lower level – PPC_2 as shown in Figure 2(b), because low environmental standards will eventually reduce the health of workers. Their decline in productive capacity may also be intensified by the high output of consumption goods, damaging the resource base and causing further species extinction (see also Table 1). Consequently, as Figure 2(b) shows, the whole range of production possibilities for both consumer goods and environmental outputs is now reduced. With an eye on the wellbeing of future generations, it might be better to locate at point B, with a higher level of environmental standards. This may be a **sustainable output** of consumer goods, leaving enough resources for the environment so as to maintain the original PPC intact. The theme of sustainable output is discussed in more detail in Chapter 4.

Whereas the PPC is, in the short run, a result of available resources and technology, *the position selected on the curve is a result of personal and collective choice*. Which point on the PPC is best? How much of its resources should the UK, or any other country, devote to the environment? The point chosen reflects nothing less than the whole range of alternatives, values, traditions and ways of looking at life which the society in question embraces. It is expressed through purchases in the marketplace and politically through the ballot box, lobbying and pressure groups.

Questions economists ask

The role of the economist is to help towards better choices by asking probing questions and providing, or encouraging the search for, relevant information on alternatives. Among the questions that economists ask are:

- What is the opportunity cost of achieving a particular environmental change?
- Is the environmental objective – for example, reducing output of

Absurdly green

Even the most fervent of anti-nuclear campaigners should oppose the Swedish government's plan to shut down two reactors. It is often ticklish to balance protection of the environment against its cost. Sweden's Social Democratic government has come up with a novel answer: a 'green' policy that is not only hugely expensive, but may actually damage the environment. It plans shortly to shut a nuclear power station that is efficient and safe; another is to be closed in 2001. If the courts permit the closures, Sweden will be poorer and dirtier – and may be more at risk from nuclear accidents.

The idea of closing down Sweden's nuclear industry emerged two decades ago, when a large majority of Swedes voted in a referendum to scrap nuclear power. But that (non-binding) vote told the government to move only gradually; no nuclear power station has yet been decommissioned. That is not fast enough for the present government. Nuclear power, it says, is dangerous: fallout from Chernobyl wafted across the country. Shutting the two stations will help boost renewable forms of energy. Admiring greens in other countries are talking of following Sweden's lead.

That would be a big mistake. Nuclear reactors are hugely expensive, both to construct and to demolish; that is the strongest argument against building any more. However, once built, they are extremely cheap to run. So it makes sense to keep them going until the end of their working lives. …

What about the environmental gains? Renewable energy is too dear and too under-developed to replace more than a fraction of the lost power. Instead, more electricity will have to be generated from coal or natural gas, which will produce more greenhouse gases, increasing global warming and also contravening the recent Kyoto protocol. Nor would shutting the stations do much to reduce Sweden's radioactive waste. Most of the waste from a nuclear power station comes from its irradiated reactor, rather than spent fuel: one more reason why, once a power station exists, it should generate electricity for as long as it is safe to do so. …Is it safe? Sweden has a good record of nuclear safety …

Swedes might retort that they are simply unwilling to stomach any nuclear danger, however minimal. But even on this basis, closing the two reactors would be wrong-headed. Several Russian and Baltic nuclear plants sell power to the Nordic electricity pool via Finland. An unintended consequence of shutting down the Swedish reactors will be to increase demand for electricity from these plants – none of which meets Swedish safety standards.

Lithuania's Ignalina plant, for instance, is one of Europe's worst – and it's several hundred miles closer to Sweden than Chernobyl. Reactors in Ukraine and Russia, only a little further off, are more dangerous still. If Swedes want to spend more money to improve their nuclear safety, it would be better to devote it to the poor and dangerous nuclear industry to their east, rather than wasting it on shutting down their own.

The Economist, 11 July 1998

CO_2, a greenhouse gas – being achieved in the most **cost-effective** way? That is to say, as cheaply as possible. Failure to be cost-effective means that the community is operating inefficiently at some point inside its PPC.

● What are the most appropriate ways of encouraging cost-effective solutions?

● How do we value environmental improvements and how do we know whether the right balance has been struck between costs and benefits?

● How do we assess environmental decisions whose impact stretches into the future?

These are some of the themes of the rest of this book. Failure to raise and answer these questions can lead to an over-zealous 'green at any price' approach (see boxed item) which is wasteful and fails to help the environmental cause. Neither dogmatism, mysticism nor fluffy philosophies to save the whales are any substitute for the questions that arise from the inescapable scarcity of resources.

KEY WORDS

Scarcity	Trade-off
Limited resources	Opportunity cost
Non-renewable resources	Sustainable output
Production possibility curve	Cost-effective
Index of environmental quality	

Reading list

Anderton, A., Unit 35 in *Economics*, 2nd edn, Causeway Press, 1995.

Grant, S., Chapter 1 in *Economic Growth and Business Cycles*, Heinemann Educational, 1999.

Grant, S., Chapter 22 in *Stanlake's Introductory Economics*, Longman, 1999.

Griffiths, A. and Wall, S. (eds), Chapter 10 in *Applied Economics*, 7th edn, Longman, 1997.

This Common Inheritance. Part 1: The Government Approach, HMSO, 1990.

Useful websites

The Countryside Council for Wales: www.ccw.gov.uk/

The European Environment Agency: www.eea.eu.int/
UK Environment Protection Agency: www.environment-agency.gov.uk/
Greenpeace: www.greenpeace.org.uk/
Friends of the Earth: www.foe.org.uk/
United States Environment Protection Agency: www.epa.gov/
United Nations Commission on Sustainable Development:
www.un.org/esa/sustdev/

Essay topics

1. (a) Explain why the concept of scarcity is important in any analysis of environmental problems. [10 marks]
   (b) Using a production possibility curve, discuss the effects of a country deciding to raise environmental standards. [15 marks]
2. (a) Explain what is meant by sustainable output. [10 marks]
   (b) Discuss whether it is desirable to reduce pollution to zero. [15 marks]

Data response question

Read the following article by Nick Nuttall, Environment Correspondent of *The Times*, which appeared on 22 March 1999. Then answer the questions that follow.

ICI heads worst list of polluters

The chemical giant ICI heads a 'Hall of Shame' of 20 companies that are the most flagrant polluters in England and Wales, the Environment Agency will announce today. Five water companies, led by Wessex, also feature in the list, along with the oil company Shell UK, several construction and waste management companies and the nuclear fuels firm BNFL.

The list is aimed at shaming industry into doing more to prevent toxic and hazardous chemicals seeping into rivers, underground aquifers and lakes, and is being used by the agency to demand tougher fines for polluters. Ed Gallagher, the agency's chief executive, said yesterday: 'Tough action in the field needs to be matched by tougher penalties being imposed by the courts. The average fine for a prosecution last year was £2786. Clearly this is not sending out a strong enough message to deter large businesses that have the potential to seriously damage the environment.'

The case of EOM Construction, which is seventh on the agency's list, underscores the agency's concern. The company was successfully prosecuted for illegally keeping and disposing of thousands of tonnes of controlled wastes on sites in Burnley and Clone. The tipping saved the company an estimated £180 000 but it was fined only £21 000 with £1 600 costs in court in November last year.

ICI's position as the most shameful company on the agency's list is based on three incidents. In March last year the company was fined £300 000 for polluting groundwater in Runcorn in Cheshire with 150 tonnes of chloroform. In June it was fined £80 000 for the accidental release of 56 tonnes of trichloroethylene, a cleaning fluid, at the same site, some of which contaminated the nearby Western Canal. ICI was also fined £2500 for allowing 200 tonnes of naphtha to escape from underground tanks at Brinefields in Cleveland, contaminating marshland and killing birds, fish and plants.

The hall of shame, which the agency plans to update annually, attracted applause from environmental groups. Friends of the Earth agreed that fines were 'pitiful'. 'ICI, who came top of the list, were fined less than 0.15 per cent of profits,' the group said. Graham Setterfield, of Water UK, which represents the water industry, said that nearly £1.5 billion had been spent over the past ten years in reducing pollution.

The hall of shame – top ten polluters in 1998:

ICI fined £328 500
Tyseley Waste Disposal fined
  £95 000
London Waste fined £38 500
Wessex Water fined £36 500
Alco Waste Management fined
  £30 000

Anglian Water Services fined
  £24 250
EOM Construction fined £21 000
Shell UK fined £20 000
BNFL fined £20 000
Celtic Energy fined £18 000

1. (a) Which types of industry figure prominently in the 'hall of shame'? [1 mark]
   (b) What types of pollution does the article mention? [2 marks]
2. Explain why the publication of a 'hall of shame' may encourage the firms to reduce pollution. [4 marks]
3. What effect do pollution fines have on private and external costs of production? [6 marks]
4. Why have pollution fines not been very effective in reducing pollution? [4 marks]
5. Assess *two* other government policy measures to reduce pollution [8 marks]

Chapter Two

Economic causes of environmental problems

'*The closed Earth of the future requires economic principles which are somewhat different from the open Earth of the past.*'
Kenneth Boulding

Introduction

Since it is so harmful, how is it that we allow environmental damage to happen? Of course, some environmental disturbance is unavoidable. Even the most basic level of human existence – breathing, eating, defecating – has an impact on our surroundings. Almost every activity from farming to travel makes demands upon, and pollutes, the environment. *Zero rates of extraction and pollution are not an answer.* The solution lies, rather, in conducting our economies and ourselves so as to minimize this impact. The ways in which this might be done are discussed in the remainder of the book. In this and the following chapters we ask an essential preliminary question: how does *avoidable* environmental damage occur in the first place?

A new model of the economy

To help us answer this we need a relevant model of the economy. The conventional circular flow model (Figure 3), familiar to students of macro-economics, shows *on the lower loop* the flow of output between producers and households; and *on the upper loop* the flow of inputs to producers.

Although this model is useful, it has a serious limitation. Even if international trade is included it is still, in a wider meaning of the term, a '*closed*' model. It takes no account of the interaction between the economy and environment on which it depends. This is also shown in Figure 3, with environmental connections added below the circular flow model.

The environment, represented in the lower part of the diagram, performs three functions:
- it provides resources
- it offers amenities
- it absorbs waste.

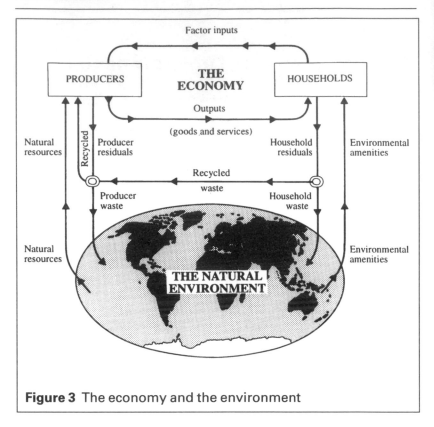

Figure 3 The economy and the environment

The flow of natural resources – minerals, water, energy, plant and animal life – from the environment to producers is shown on the extreme left of the diagram. This flow contributes in turn to the output of goods and services going to households. On the far right of the diagram we see, flowing directly to households, environmental amenities in the form of country walks, pleasant views and the opportunity for other recreational activities. Producers and households generate 'leftovers' or residuals, some of which are recycled to contribute once more to the flow of output. The remainder are dumped in the environment – labelled 'producer and household waste' in the diagram.

The three functions of the environment – as a provider of resources and of amenities and as an absorber of waste – interact with each other, sometimes in a competitive way and sometimes in a complementary way. Water is a good illustration of this.

The data in the boxed item opposite show competing claims on water use in the UK. We can summarize the problem with a simple

UK WATER DEMANDS

For manufacturing and processing
- One ton of aluminium requires 300 000 gallons.
- A four-door family car requires 100 000 gallons.
- One bag of coke requires 3000 gallons.

For households
- Two-thirds of the 3.8 billion gallons used daily in England and Wales is accounted for by domestic users. Domestic water consumption breaks down as follows:

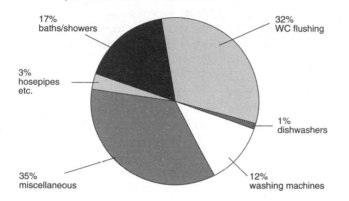

17% baths/showers

32% WC flushing

3% hosepipes etc.

1% dishwashers

35% miscellaneous

12% washing machines

As a waste receiver
- 80 per cent by weight of all waste in England and Wales is liquid effluent dispersed partly to seas and estuaries but mainly to rivers. 'The most important medium for receiving, processing and transporting liquid effluents' – Royal Commission on Environmental Pollution.

As an amenity
- 'The provision of amenity service is the third economic function of the environment. Thus in the UK the government has imposed a duty on the Environment Agency and the water companies to:

   – 'conserve and enhance natural beauty and conserve flora, fauna and geological features of special interest'
   – 'ensure that water and land are made available for recreation'.

Sources: Welsh Water plc; Water Services Association

hypothetical example. The Rubicon River, as it flows into a populated area, provides water for industrial, agricultural and domestic services; this same water is discharged back into the Rubicon as effluent; and citizens of Rubiconia City like to spend their leisure time engaging in water sports and fishing. There is a limit to the capacity of the Rubicon to fulfil any one of these functions and it may be further reduced by its use for other purposes. Whether or not these uses are mutually exclusive will frequently depend on the level of use and the level of water in the river. High rates of effluent discharged, especially when the river level is low, would mean that for some purposes the water of the Rubicon could not be used as production input and it would certainly reduce its amenity services. When the river level is high, however, its ability to break down and absorb a given level of waste is increased and the diluted effluent is no longer a serious threat to other functions.

The spaceship economy

The new model, which incorporates the interaction between the economy and the environment, helps us to see more clearly why things go wrong. In both our imaginary example and in reality, a river may become poisoned with waste; reduced to a sluggish trickle through excessive water use, or become so crowded with recreational users that it ceases to be enjoyable. Figure 3 shows why the river, or any other environmental resource, is misused. The vital links between the economy and the environment in the diagram are, for reasons explained in the following sections, somehow forgotten or overlooked, *so decisions taken in the economy about making the best use of resources pay little regard to the environment.*

Because the environmental links do not appear in market prices, in the balance sheets of producers, or in the calculations of national income, we tend to regard the environment as if it were a free resource. In an influential article 'The Coming Spaceship Earth', the American economist Kenneth Boulding claimed that many of our environmental problems arose because we tended to treat the world as a 'cowboy economy' with a limitless 'wild west' frontier of resources available for reckless exploitation. By contrast, as we come to realize our impact on the environment, we should think of our planet '*as a spaceship, without unlimited reservoirs of anything, either for extraction or for pollution*'.

Market failure

The great advantage of markets, when they are working properly, is that they ensure an efficient use of scarce resources. Markets generate

THERMODYNAMICS

Central to the view of the earth as a system with limited resources is the famous *First Law of Thermodynamics,* which states that energy and matter cannot be created or destroyed. In terms of our new model this implies that, if we wish to reduce the polluting mass of waste disposed of in the natural environment, the options open to us might be to:

- produce fewer goods and services
- reduce the amount of residuals generated in the production and use of goods and services
- increase recycling.

Energy cannot be destroyed, but the *Second Law of Thermodynamics* (entropy) tells us what happens – it is dissipated or transformed. The economy draws upon usable, low-entropy materials – minerals and fuel – from the environment. In turn, manufacturing and consumption generate less usable (sometimes useless) higher-entropy waste products, gases and wasted heat. This reminds us that, despite the scope for recycling, it can never be completely successful. Recycling itself uses energy and creates further waste. *100 per cent recycling is not economically feasible or socially desirable.*

There are three sets of economic reasons why in mixed economies (government sector plus private markets) we manage to ignore the lessons of thermodynamics and overlook the links between the economy and the environment:

- **market failure** (discussed in this chapter)
- **missing markets** (discussed in Chapter 3)
- **government failure** (discussed in Chapter 3).

information on scarcity, which is signalled in the form of prices. At the same time, prices provide powerful incentives to act on this information, as suppliers of capital and labour, in seeking to avoid losses and maximize income, try to make best use of their resources.

Nevertheless, the wasteful destruction of scarce environmental resources is an example of a **market failure.** Whenever a price becomes distorted or misleading, so that it does not provide a true signal of the underlying forces of supply and demand, then market failure occurs. Too much or too little is produced. The artificially high prices caused by monopolies are just one example.

Here we are concerned with the impact on the environment of market failure caused by *externalities*. These are so named because they are costs (called **negative externalities** or **external costs**), or benefits (**positive externalities** or **external benefits**), which extend beyond – and are therefore *external* to – the actions of a particular supplier or consumer. Thus the act of one household or firm imposes external costs or confers external benefits on another household or firm. These external costs or benefits are not transmitted through prices.

Both positive and negative externalities can arise between producers, between consumers, or between producers and consumers, as shown in Table 2 opposite.

Negative externalities

Figure 4 illustrates a negative externality. It might, for example, be the cost of acid rain, damaging to forestry and fishing, created by sulphur dioxide fumes from coal-fired power stations. The acid rain damage is shown as MEC, the marginal external cost curve – the damage caused

---

DIRTY WASHING

The effect of smoke from a factory chimney was one of the earliest textbook cases of a negative externality: quoted by the economist A.C. Pigou, whose pioneering study *Economics of Welfare* was published in 1920. Based on an actual investigation in Manchester in 1914, this showed that households in the vicinity of the factory incurred costs of £290 000, caused by soot falling on washing hanging out to dry.

Today, in an era of washing machines, we would concentrate on studying the more injurious effects of emissions listed in Table 2. However, the principle which Pigou identified applies to all cases of pollution: the difference between **private costs** (in this case the cost of manufacturing and of inputs purchased by the factory) and **social costs** (the total cost to the community of the factory output). This should include the external cost of £290 000 for laundry bills. Because the laundry costs are external to the firm, they are not included in its bills or cost accounts – and therefore in the price it charges.

Private cost + external cost = social cost.

Remember that the so-called private costs must be included because the resources the factory output absorbs are not available to the wider community for any alternative use.

Table 2 Examples of environmental externalities

	Negative (cost)	Positive (benefit)
Consumer to consumer	• Car exhaust fumes/noise • Traffic congestion • Street litter, especially from take-aways	• Well-kept gardens are a pleasure to passers-by and raise the value of adjacent properties
Producer to producer	• A crop spray used on a potato farm which also kills insects that pollinate fruit trees in neighbouring orchards • Depletion of fish stocks	• A farmer improving land drainage may at the same time improve adjacent land on other farms
Producer to consumer	• Any waste or emission dumped or discharged in the environment without taking account of the external costs	• Any pleasant aroma from a coffee or chocolate factory, perfumery or bakery

by an extra unit of output. The curve is upward sloping, as for most types of pollution, because the forests and fisheries become worse at an assumed that the power stations have a fixed technology and can only alter emissions by reducing output.

The supply curve, assuming a perfectly competitive industry, is S, which is derived from the horizontal sum of the marginal private cost curves (MPC) of the firms in the industry. The demand curve D is, at the same time, also a measure of how much the community is willing to pay for an extra unit of output from the power stations – the marginal social benefit (MSB = D). The competitive industry produces the output which maximizes profits, where supply is equal to demand – output Q_c at price P_c. From a social viewpoint, this price is too low and the output too high. It takes no account of the external costs. To do this we must add MEC to S (putting MEC on top of the S curve). We then get a full measure of marginal social costs – the MSC curve.

$$MSC = MEC + MPC.$$

The **socially efficient output** (which can also be called the socially optimum output) is at the point where the price P_s of the product is equal to the marginal social cost of production at output Q_s. This is efficient because at this point the extra cost of the extra or marginal

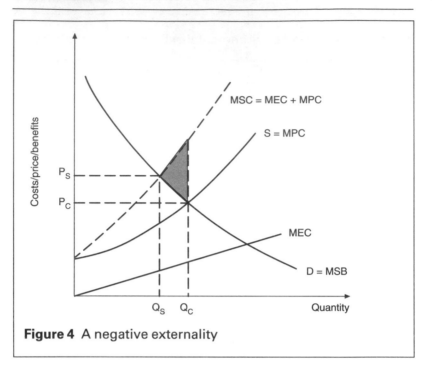

Figure 4 A negative externality

unit of output, including environmental costs, is just equal to what the community thinks it is worth – its price, P_s = MSC. But the competitive industry produces an output Q_c at which point the price P_c is less than the MSC. This tells us that output is too high and too much sulphur dioxide is being discharged into the atmosphere.

The cost of the inefficiency is the shaded area – all units of output for which MSC exceeds MSB (known as **welfare triangle loss**). This is a loss without any compensating gains, and represents the full costs associated with that part of the output between Q_s and Q_c for which the community is not prepared to pay. Nevertheless, it is inflicted on the community because the price P_c is too low – hiding the external cost. The efficient level of output is at Q_s at a price P_s.

Positive externalities

Figure 5 shows how the consequences of positive externalities may be a level of output which is too low, and takes the example of a home-owner's garden.

The marginal cost curve for the investment of time and money in gardening is horizontal because the extra (or marginal) costs to the house-holder of planting an extra bed of flowers, it is assumed, will not

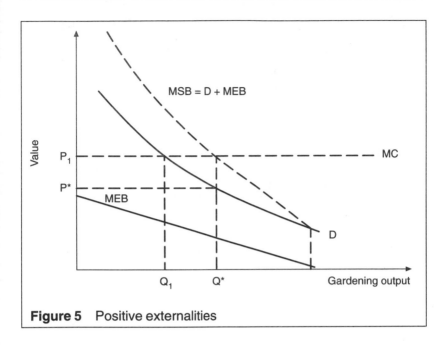

Figure 5 Positive externalities

be affected by the amount of gardening done. The pleasant garden generates external benefits to neighbours and passers-by, as the marginal external benefit curve (MEB) shows. This curve is likely to be down-wards sloping in this case, because the marginal benefit may be large for small improvements to a very untidy garden, but less significant as further work is done.

The marginal social benefit (MSB) curve is calculated by adding the **marginal private benefit** and the marginal external benefit together – putting the MEB curve on top of the demand curve D. Thus:

$$MSB = MPB + MEB.$$

The efficient level of output Q^* is at the point where the marginal social benefit to the community of an 'extra unit' of gardening improvements is equal to the marginal cost of the work. This is where the MC and MSB curves intersect. The inefficiency occurs because the home-owner does not manage to reap all the benefits from the invest-ment in the garden improvements. Passers-by cannot be charged for the benefit they derive from pleasant gardens, nor then is there any way of reaping the gains from the impact on other property values. Consequently the price P_1 is too high to achieve the appropriate level

23

of garden maintenance for the neighbourhood. The efficient price would be P*, a pleasing thought for gardeners.

Suburban gardens may seem a trivial example, compared with worldwide environmental problems, but the principle established here has wider implications. *Wherever a positive externality occurs, not enough resources or effort will be directed towards producing the right amount of the good or activity which generates the positive externality.*

Remedies
How can market failure caused by externalities be remedied? This is discussed in more detail in Chapters 7, 8 and 9. Here we briefly note two possibilities.

Regulations
Regulations could be imposed by the government restricting output to Q_s in Figure 4 – this is known as a **command and control system** (CAC).

A market incentive approach
This involves using the price signal to obtain the socially efficient output. This could be achieved by a tax on the polluting output (originally proposed by Pigou – hence the **Pigouvian tax**). If the tax raises the price from P_c to P_s, output is reduced to the desired level Q_s. The Pigouvian tax is a measure which is consistent with the **polluter pays principle** (PPP) – the idea that the price should include all external environmental costs. A sound idea this may be, but put into practice in the form advocated by its most enthusiastic supporters it could lead to some controversially high prices – for example, £138 for a hamburger (see boxed item). Read this now and *try the following questions when you have read Chapter 3:*

● How does this article illustrate both government and market failure?
● What economic principle is being proposed here?
● What are the practical problems of such an idea?

Human action inevitably causes some environmental disturbance and damage. However, much of the environmental destruction that occurs is unnecessary and avoidable. It arises in part because of the failure of markets to provide the right price signals so as to minimize the environmentally harmful effects of pollution and consumption (negative externalities), or to encourage the good effects (positive externalities).

Why a hamburger should cost $200

NANCY DUNNE

Ecologists ... believe the world's trade ministers can only tinker with an economic system that is fundamentally flawed by its failure to count the ecological costs of production. 'This could leave us with a world where there's lots of money but dirty air and water and environmental degradation,' says Alan Thein Durning, author of *Saving the Forests: What Will it Take?* from the Worldwatch Institute, an environmental group. What is needed is a system of 'full-cost pricing' that includes environmental costs in production of goods, he says. This would radically alter cost structures.

A mature forest tree in India would then be worth $50,000 (£34,000), according to the Centre for Science and Environment in New Delhi. A hamburger produced on pasture cleared from rain forests would cost $200. One hectare of a Malaysian forest, providing carbon storage services and helping to prevent climate change, would be worth more than $3,000 over the long term, according to Durning.

Environmentalists fear the costs of not moving towards ecological pricing will only become clear after it is too late. Deforestation is accelerating; two-thirds of the planet's original forests have already disappeared.

Political reform is also necessary to reforestation efforts. 'To varying degrees, a bond between timber money and political power is found in all the world's main timber economies,' says Durning. 'In less democratic societies, those who question the prerogatives of economic power all too often end up as murder statistics in human rights reports.'

Durning alleges that in countries like Malaysia – the world's largest exporter of tropical timber – elected leaders distribute to their loyal supporters contracts for the exploitation of public resources. Even in the US, the government moves reluctantly against the entrenched timber, mining and beef interests.

He would like full-cost pricing phased in over 10–20 years through user fees, green taxes and tariffs. He reckons that a $3-a-day charge to visitors to US national forests would raise more money than timber sales from US government-owned lands.

But first, governments must stop subsidizing forest destruction. In the US the Clinton administration is edging towards raising prices for grazing lands, mining resources and, eventually, timber sales.

No country can move to full cost pricing alone without risking having their industries undercut by foreign producers whose governments do not make environmental destruction costly. Global action is necessary.

Financial Times, 12 January 1994

In addition to market failure we must consider the problems created by missing markets and government failure, which are discussed in the following chapter.

KEY WORDS

Market failure	Social costs
Missing markets	Socially efficient output
Negative externalities	Welfare triangle loss
External costs	Private benefit
Positive externalities	Command/control system
External benefits	Pigouvian tax
Private costs	Polluter pays principle

Reading list
Anderton, A., Unit 36 in *Economics*, 2nd edn, Causeway Press, 1995.
Bamford, C., Chapter 3 in *Transport Economics*, 2nd edn, Heinemann Educational, 1998.
Maunder, P., Myers, D., Wall, N. and Miller, R., Chapter 10 in *Economics Explained,* 3rd edn, Collins Educational, 1995.
Wilkinson, M., Chapter 3 in *Equity and Efficiency*, Heinemann Educational, 1993.

Useful websites
Greenpeace: www.greenpeace.org.uk/
Friends of the Earth: www.foe.org.uk/

Essay topics
1. (a) Define, and give examples of, external costs and benefits. [10 marks]
   (b) Discuss whether it is possible to achieve an optimal allocation of resources of externalities. [10 marks]
2. (a) Distinguish, with the aid of examples, between positive externalities and negative externalities. [10 marks]
   (b) Discuss the extent to which subsidies to producers are the best means for a government to encourage the consumption of goods and services that generate positive externalities. [15 marks]

Data response question

This task is based on a specimen question set by the University of Cambridge Local Examinations Syndicate as a specimen question in 1997. Read the extract, which is adapted from an article in the *Yorkshire Evening Post* on 1 February 1990. Then answer the questions.

A market for waste paper

A waste paper recycling scheme run by Leeds City Council which has raised thousands of pounds for charity could be forced to close – by the success of the 'green' revolution.

The price of waste paper has dropped by nearly 60 per cent since September of last year – from £12 to £5 per tonne. It costs the council an average of £6 per tonne to run and administer the scheme.

That means the council's 'Save Waste and Prosper' (SWAP) scheme, which raised £20 000 for charity last year, is now having to pay £1 for every tonne it collects because the price of waste paper has dropped as a result of an increase in waste paper being recycled by environmentally conscious householders. There has been no change in the demand for waste paper from industry.

Some charity groups have abandoned their waste schemes because it is no longer worth their while to collect old newspapers.

SWAP chairman Liz Minkin admitted that the long-term future of the council's collection service was in jeopardy unless the Government introduced legislation to reduce the waste paper surplus. Councillor Minkin said the printing and newspaper industries should be forced to use more recycled paper in their products and that the market was in danger of collapse without regulation.

Operations Manager Peter Jackson said it would cost the authority about £17 per tonne to bury waste paper in waste disposal sites.

1. With reference to the information provided, use demand and supply diagrams to show how the market for waste paper changed from September 1989 to February 1990. [5 marks]
2. Economists identify three types of costs and benefits in the production of goods and services: private, external and social.
   (i) Distinguish between these three. (ii) Using the information provided as required, analyse the costs and benefits of the recycling scheme. [3, 6 marks]
3. Councillor Minkin believes that regulation is needed to encourage the printing and newspaper industries to use more recycled paper and so reduce the stocks of waste paper. What *other* policies might an economist recommend to achieve the same objectives? [6 marks]

Chapter Three

Efficient pollution, missing markets and government failure

The phrase 'efficient pollution' enrages some greens and further convinces them that economists are completely insensitive to the environment.

The phrase **'efficient pollution'** appears to contain a contradiction because pollution is clearly harmful and it might seem absurd to imagine that it could also be efficient. Yet this is simply a statement about making best use of scarce resources. As Figure 4 on page 22 showed, even at the socially efficient level of output Q_s, some pollution from sulphur emissions will occur. This is not surprising since zero pollution would require no production, which might be quite unacceptable.

What is the efficient level of pollution? This can be seen more clearly from Figure 6(a) which just concentrates on the costs of the damage done by the pollution and the cost of reducing it (**abatement costs**). That includes the cost of pollution control equipment; the cost of inspection and the value of any output forgone in reducing emissions. The **marginal cost of abatement** (MCA) curve shows the extra cost of abatement arising from the reduction in pollution by one unit – measured here by the level of emissions. To understand the diagram, consider a movement from right to left – a reduction in pollution levels.

The steepness of the MCA curve will vary according to the type of pollutant. The MCA curve for reducing wastes discharged into a river, for example, will be different from that for lowering emissions of sulphur dioxide into the atmosphere. Nevertheless, the extra (or marginal) cost of extra reductions in pollution can be expected to rise as more valuable resources are drawn into further abatement. The marginal cost may become very high at low levels of pollution. Increasing the quality of river water from 85 to 95 per cent purity, it has been estimated, *may double abatement costs*. Similarly, totally litter-free streets, requiring a warden on every street corner, may be prohibitively expensive.

The **marginal social cost of pollution** (MSCP) curve measures the costs created by an increase in pollution of one unit – a movement to the right on the diagram. It is the same as the MEC curve of Figure 4,

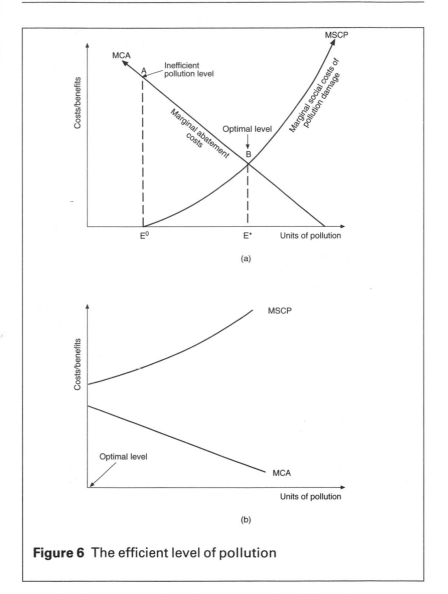

Figure 6 The efficient level of pollution

but relabelled to remind us that we are only talking about marginal social costs arising from pollution. The MSCP curve is sometimes zero up to a certain pollution level because of the capacity of the environment to absorb waste – by natural dispersion, by wind, water and bio-degradation.

The socially efficient level of pollution is at E^*, where the marginal

29

social cost of pollution is equal to the marginal social cost of abatement. If emissions were reduced further, to E_0, then the total abatement cost of reducing pollution from E^* to E_0 is represented by the area E^*E_0AB. The value of reducing the damage done by this pollution, and hence the value to the community for reducing it, is the area E^*E_0B. The costs of this reduction exceeds the benefit by E_0AB – a net loss for the community. *Any point to the left of E^* will be an inefficiently high level of pollution reduction since the marginal cost to the community will exceed the marginal benefit.*

The case of lethal pollutants, which are potentially threatening on a worldwide scale, such as plutonium or CFCs, is shown in Figure 6(b). Here the MSCP is above the abatement cost curve at every level of emission. *In this case the efficient level of pollution is zero, at zero output.*

Missing markets

How exactly do the problems associated with externalities arise? If each firm had to pay to emit fumes into the atmosphere, then socially efficient decisions would be made. But since no one owns the atmosphere, there is no market and therefore no market price for clean air to guide businesses' and consumers' decisions. Firms have every incentive to pollute because clean air is mistakenly regarded as a *free good* with a price of zero.

Property rights

The connection between missing markets and the absence of property rights was first analysed by the Nobel Prize winning economist, Ronald Coase. If resources are not owned, they will be wasted because no price will be charged for their use. Coase argued that if property rights are well defined, individuals will benefit by bargaining for use of the scarce resources – **Coase bargaining** as it is sometimes called – thus creating a market.

This internalizes the externality which is included in the market price and ensures an efficient outcome. A possible answer to environmental problems, it is claimed, would be to extend and clearly define property rights in all natural resources. The scope for this is examined in Chapter 8.

The problems created by the absence of property rights can be shown in the following example. If fishermen have unlimited access to waters which nobody owns (Figure 7), each trawler will catch fish at a rate of C_1 and where marginal private cost (MPC) is equal to demand – assuming perfect competition in the fishing industry. If competition and modern technology cause the total catch of fish to rise beyond the

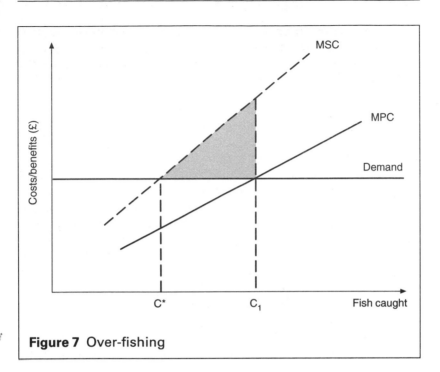

Figure 7 Over-fishing

natural replenishment level, stocks of fish and the fishing industry will eventually cease to exist. Although this is recognized, each individual firm feels that its catch is too small to make any difference. Competing trawlers will try to catch as many fish as possible while stocks last, so creating an externality by contributing to the extinction of the stock.

The marginal social cost curve (MSC), which includes the external costs of excessive fishing, indicates that the socially efficient level of catch would be C^*, where MSC equals demand. Individual trawlers, ignoring external cost, catch too many fish at C_1. The shaded area represents the external cost of over-fishing. If the property rights in the fishery were created and placed in the hands of a single owner, the problem might be solved. It is in the owner's interest to charge a fee to fishermen equal to the marginal social cost of fishing. This reduces the catch to C^*, which preserves stocks and the industry.

A practical problem arising from the solution suggested above is to exclude fishermen who don't pay. This might be feasible with the private ownership of a small river or lake, but impossible for the single owner of a vast resource such as an ocean. Some form of international co-operation with government regulation of the fishing industry may be necessary.

31

The difficulty of *exclusion* is common to what are known as **public goods.** A public good is a type of good that may be supplied by private enterprise or the public sector, but usually has to be financed by the public sector. With a **private good,** such as ice cream, people who don't pay can be *excluded.* Also, consumption is rival – one person's ice cream consumption means less for others. By contrast a public good, such as a lighthouse, is *non-rival* – an extra ship does not affect the availability of light for other ships. It is also *non-excludable* – no vessel can be denied the benefit of the light.

The quality of the environment is also a form of public good. If, for example, the purity of air is improved in an industrial area, everyone benefits because no one can be excluded. But if we depended on the voluntary payments to secure clean air, people would be tempted to become **free-riders,** relying on the payments of others. Consequently, a private firm undertaking to purify the air will probably not earn enough revenue to cover the costs.

It follows from this that *private markets, if left entirely to themselves, are likely to under-supply environmental quality.* Although there is demand for, and a capacity to supply, environmental goods, the necessary markets are incomplete or missing. Some form of collective finance through taxation rather than individual voluntary payments may be necessary.

Congestion and public goods

When the use of a public good approaches capacity – a crowded national park or road network for example – it ceases to be non-rival. It becomes an **'impure' public good,** with rival consumption, one of the features of a private good. Well below full capacity, an extra walker or motorist will have no effect on the consumption of other users. Also in terms of wear and tear, the marginal cost caused by extra use is virtually zero. Apart from the exclusion problem, this is often seen as a justification for not charging for public goods. Economic efficiency requires that marginal cost (zero in this case) equals price.

However, at peak times each extra walker or motorist, by adding to congestion, reduces the utility of others, so creating a marginal cost quite distinct from wear and tear. This is shown in Figure 8. At off-peak times, the marginal cost (MC) and average cost (AC) of travelling, measured in driving time, are equal. Beyond traffic volume V_1, congestion increases, as each extra driver inflicts a time delay on others. Since average cost (journey time) is rising, marginal cost is higher than average cost. Fuel costs also rise. A small car, for example, travelling at an average speed

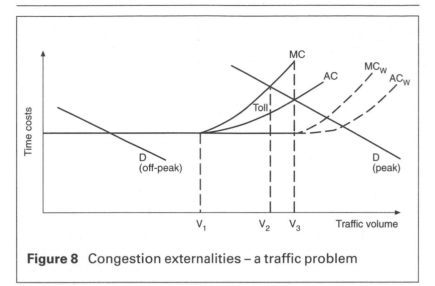

Figure 8 Congestion externalities – a traffic problem

of 27 mph costs nearly three pence a mile extra in congested traffic when its speed is reduced to 17 mph. The efficient volume of traffic is V_2, where peak demand (marginal social benefit) is equal to marginal cost; that is, MSB = MC.

Because this marginal cost, known as a **congestion externality**, is borne by other motorists, each driver is only interested in average journey time. Consequently demand increases to V_3 – an excessively congested and inefficient level of traffic, where marginal social cost exceeds marginal social benefit. A road widening scheme will reduce journey time but may create congestion externalities once again at an even higher volume of traffic as demand expands (dotted MC_W and AC_W in Figure 8). For example, the London orbital road (M25) was designed for about 80 thousand cars a day; but now its busiest section (in the south-west) carries up to 200 thousand a day.

This is another example of a missing market and missing market price, which is needed to internalize the congestion externality and bring marginal social cost into equality with marginal social benefit. A charge or toll for peak-period use could be the answer. This principle, subject to a satisfactory solution to the exclusion problem, can be applied to national parks, or any shared environmental resource where congestion externalities arise.

Government failure

So far we have identified environmental problems created by market failures. Can governments do any better? Disappointingly, govern-

33

ment policies and activities, as a side-effect, can cause significant environmental damage:

- *In developed countries* there is sometimes conflict between environmental interests and government intervention to support farmers' incomes. The EU common agricultural policy, for example, intended to stabilize farm incomes and output, has increased the use of environmentally damaging pesticides and fertilizers. It has also encouraged the destruction of wildlife habitats such as small woodlands and hedgerows.

- *In developing countries* governments intervene with subsidies and controls – bringing prices below the market level – to assist the poor and promote economic development. These artificially low prices give the wrong signals, encouraging wasteful use of, for example, scarce energy and water resources. Although owned by governments, tropical rain forests are being destroyed, by concessions granted to commercial timber companies and peasant farmers, using the slash-and-burn method to clear land.

- *In command economies*, which replace markets by government controls, the record is even worse. The former Soviet Union, for example, now moving towards a market economy, is an environmentalist's nightmare. This is the legacy of the system which emphasized the achievement of planned output targets with little regard for consumers or the environment. Dissenting green views were suppressed. *Coase-style bargaining* between polluter and pollutees, to internalize environmental externalities, was unknown. Planners' targets ruled.

All of the problems noted above occur because governments fail to take account of the indirect environmental effects of their policies. Like market failures, government failures are also avoidable if corrective action is taken. This can be achieved by:

- ensuring that environmental standards are not overlooked by any government departments
- a systematic evaluation of all positive and negative externalities before starting any programme of government expenditure or legislation.

The latter provides a check on whether a proposed course of action is worthwhile – if the necessary social benefits exceed or are equal to social costs.

Summing up

The causes of environmental damage arise from a combination of related factors:

- externalities
- the lack of well-defined property rights
- the environment having characteristics of public goods.

These factors contribute to incomplete or missing markets. In turn these generate misleading prices, or no price at all, to guide producers and consumers towards socially efficient choices about the environment. To this list of causes we can add government failure.

However, many would assert that the major threat to the environment comes not from missing markets or from governments but from the pursuit of ever-increasing living standards or, less ambitiously, simply supporting an increasing world population. It is claimed that the higher output that this requires must involve the continuing destruction of natural resources. *Can we have economic growth and at the same time save the environment?* That is the theme of the next chapter.

KEY WORDS

Efficient pollution	Public goods
Abatement costs	Private goods
Marginal cost of abatement	Free-riders
Marginal social cost of pollution	Impure public goods
	Congestion externality
Missing markets	Government failure
Coase bargaining	

Reading list

Bamford, C., Chapter 6 in *Transport Economics*, 2nd edn, Heinemann Educational, 1998.

Beardshaw, J., Brewster, D., Cormack, P. and Ross, A., Chapter 24 in *Economics: A Student's Guide*, 4th edn, Addison-Wesley Longman, 1998.

Economics and Business Education Association, Unit 6 in *Core Economics*, Heinemann Educational, 1995.

Wilkinson, M., Chapters 5 and 6 in *Equity and Efficiency*, Heinemann Educational, 1993.

Useful websites
DETR on roads: www.roads.detr.gov.uk/roadnetwork/heta/sactra98.htm
US Environmental Protection Agency: www.epa.gov/

Essay topics
1. (a) What are the social costs and benefits involved in the use of private cars? [10 marks]
   (b) Discuss whether government intervention designed to reduce traffic congestion will always improve the situation. [15 marks]
2. (a) Distinguish between a private and a public good. [10 marks]
   (b) Discuss whether the following are private or public goods: (i) defence, (ii) education, (iii) air purity, (iv) roads. [15 marks]

Data response question
This task is based on a question set by the University of London Examinations and Assessment Council in 1997. Study all the data relating to transport and then answer the questions that follow.

Figure A   Spending on rail infrastructure, 1993

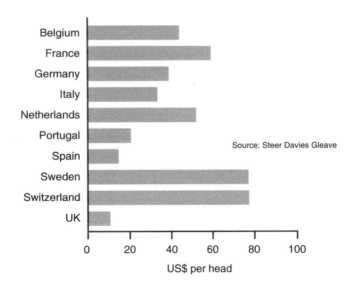

Figure B Road traffic growth, billion vehicle – km per year, UK

Figure C Passenger transport, billion passenger – km per year, UK

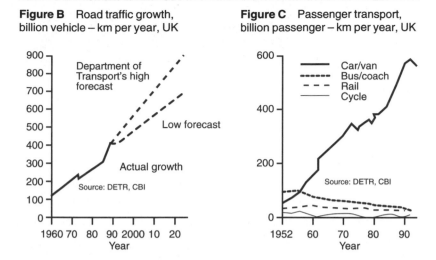

Figure D Road transport costs and revenue, 1993

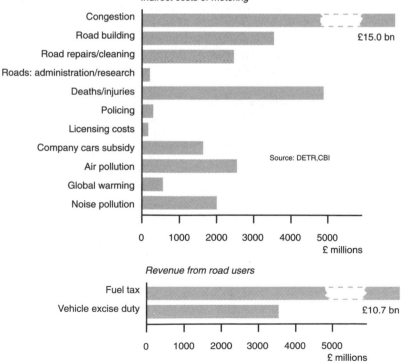

Table A Passenger transport price indices for the UK

	1981	1986	1991	1994	1995
Fares and other travel costs	100	135	186	219	n/a
Bus and coach fares	100	139	198	242	252
Rail fares	100	137	201	241	246
Other	100	107	136	155	157
Motoring costs	100	131	163	196	n/a
Purchase of vehicles	100	116	144	158	161
Maintenance of vehicles	100	138	195	239	242
Petrol and oil	100	145	156	191	202
Vehicle tax and insurance	100	146	220	320	320
Retail price index (all items)	100	137	185	201	208

Source: *Social Trends*, HMSO, 1996

1. (a) With reference to the data, how might the changing pattern of transport use in the UK be explained? [8 marks]
   (b) What other information would you find useful in explaining these changes? [4 marks]
2. (a) With reference to Figure D, how does the use of private cars give rise to external costs? [4 marks]
   (b) To what extent do the taxes levied on road users compensate for the external costs of motoring? [3 marks]
3. (a) Examine *one* policy which might be used to reduce the growth of road traffic in the next 20 years. [6 marks]

Chapter Four

Sustainable development

'*... development that meets the needs of the present without compromising the ability of future generations to meet their own needs.*' World Commission on Environment and Development, 1987 – the Bruntland Report

The issues

Can the output of goods and services be raised to match increasing demand without damaging the environment? The demand comes not only from rising world population, but also from rising expectations of higher living standards. Worldwide we see the challenge to traditional values – the expectation that people should be better off and better educated than their grandparents or parents.

The pursuit of higher living standards now may result in a permanent lowering of living standards in the future. As Chapters 1–3 have indicated, this might happen because:

- we exhaust the world's natural resources
- we exceed its capacity to act as a sink for waste.

What are the implications of this for growth of the gross domestic product (GDP)? Some argue that, since it is productive activities and certain forms of consumption which contribute to pollution, growth in GDP should be reduced. Others even advocate a zero growth rate in GDP. Against this there is the view that zero growth is no solution, because we would have fewer resources to clean up the present environmental problems created by past growth. Its supporters claim that increasing the growth rate of GDP would actually contribute to the solution of environmental problems, instead of causing them.

The economist's response to this is that both the zero-growth and maximum-growth supporters miss the point – pollution may be the result of the **misallocation of resources** rather than growth itself. Whatever its growth rate, a community can be engaged in environmentally damaging production and consumption activities. As explained in the previous chapter, this can occur because of externalities and 'missing markets', together with the absence of well defined property rights in the environment. As a result, inputs are wasted and goods and services produced without regard for their true cost.

The origins of sustainable development

Instead of a sterile argument over growth rates, environmentalists now find it more useful to ask:

- What conditions are necessary for **sustainable development**?
- How can we manage growth so that it does not destroy the resources – natural assets and manufactured assets – on which it depends?

The idea of sustainable development, with its stress on environmental management or 'good husbandry', is not new. First introduced by the forestry industry almost a century ago, it re-emerged as a key issue in environmental economics in the 1980s, amid the growing concern about the degradation of natural resources. It was put firmly on the international agenda in 1987 by the influential United Nations' World Commission on Environment and Development, in its report *Our Common Future*. Popularly known as the Bruntland Report (after its chairperson, Mrs G.H. Bruntland, prime minister of Norway), it emphasized:

- meeting the essential needs of the world's poor – jobs, food, energy, water and sanitation
- unification of economics and ecology in decision-making at all levels
- the need to promote and improve the quality of development while conserving and enhancing the resource base
- effective citizen participation in decision-making
- ensuring a sustainable level of population
- an international system which fosters sustainable patterns of trade and development.

Key ingredients of 'sustainable development'

Defining sustainable development is not easy, because it is a debatable concept involving – as the list above indicates – ethical judgements regarding what is right and fair, about which people will disagree. Twenty-four definitions are listed in Pearce's *Blueprint for a Green Economy*. Perhaps the most widely accepted definition is the one used in the Bruntland Report quoted at the head of this chapter. Below we review the meanings behind the words in the quotation and the various ways in which it has been interpreted in the sustainable development debate:

Development

Whereas **economic growth** refers to any increase in real GDP, **development** means improved living standards – *either*:

- an increase in GDP or consumption per capita, *or*
- an improvement in the quality of life, not only in terms of personal consumption, but including measures of health, education, leisure, social life and the environment.

A less ambitious view of sustainable development is simply 'non-declining consumption' (or quality of life) per capita. In this case the increase in resources would match but not exceed population growth.

Needs
In contrast to the standard economic definition of demand – willingness and ability to buy at specified prices – the use of the word 'needs' implies an ethical view about essential community and individual requirements, which must in fairness be satisfied. The Bruntland Report distinguished between 'essential needs' and 'perceived needs', which it saw as being socially and culturally determined. It warned that the satisfaction of perceived needs today may well prevent future generations from satisfying their essential needs.

Present and future generations
The reference in the quotation to the needs of present and future generations is concerned with two aspect of fairness, or equity: **intragenerational equity** (within generations) and **inter-generational equity** (between generations).

The significance of *intra-generational equity* for environmental issues lies in the fact that it is the world's poor in the north as well as the south who suffer most from environmental degradation but who make the least demand on environmental resources. Furthermore, it is the poorest of the world who rely most heavily on such natural assets as fuel wood; on vegetation for human consumption; on clothing and shelter; on wild animals and fish for protein and their dung and bones for fertilizer; and on untreated water supplies. The more these resources are depleted and degraded, the more people in the Third World will come to depend on technological substitutes and the greater the responsibility of the developed world to make this technology possible.

Consider the following statistics:

- The USA has 5 per cent of the world's population. It uses 25 per cent of the world's energy and emits 22 per cent of all carbon dioxide.
- India has 16 per cent of the world's population. It uses 3 per cent of the world's energy and emits 3 per cent of all carbon dioxide.
- The USA produces 25 per cent of world GDP (at market exchange rates) whereas India produces 1 per cent.

The question of *inter-generational equity* arises because the present generation derives benefits from using the environment as a resource base and waste sink, but the costs of such use are passed on to future generations. The most obvious example today is the nuclear energy industry, which is creating radioactive waste that will be extremely hazardous for a thousand years without having developed a safe system for handling it.

There are two broad views about how this time-separation of costs and benefits can be dealt with.

- The first requires that future generations are protected only from catastrophe, into which category fall global warming and ozone depletion. There the responsibility would end, and the resource depletion, species distinction, etc., would be tolerated for the benefit of the present generation, whilst future generations would have to cope as best they could with whatever they inherited.
- The second, more demanding interpretation, requires that future generations are enabled to enjoy the same levels of environmental consumption as the present generation. However, there are difficulties involved in specifying exactly what should be inherited (the stock of assets).

The stock of assets

If the present generation is not to deprive future generations of resources to satisfy their needs, then it should pass on a stock of assets no smaller than the one it inherited. This stock, or portfolio, of assets comprises:

> natural capital (renewable and non-renewable)
> + manufactured capital
> + human capital (skills and knowledge).

The aim of keeping this stock of assets intact is to maintain a sustainable flow of income. It will not be sustainable in the long run if, in the short run, it is boosted by depreciating the stock – for example, failing to repair worn-out equipment or to replant trees.

Should the stock of assets passed on to future generations be identical to that which we inherit – a constant portfolio? Clearly the idea of constancy is irrelevant with non-renewable resources (minerals and fossil fuels), since depletion is a consequence of use. In this case, the issue becomes one of substitutability between natural and manufactured assets. For example, some would argue that the complete exhaustion of fossil fuels and their replacement by solar energy technology is consistent with sustainable development. Good environmental management would require that non-renewable resources are not depleted before replacement technologies are developed or alternative mineral/fuel deposits are located.

Does substitutability also apply to the *renewable* (plants and animals) part of the natural asset stock? Would it be possible – or desirable – to pass on to the next generation a stock of assets whose composition has been changed – substituting manufactured for natural assets – but whose productive capacity is the same as that of the stock of assets originally inherited? For example, are smaller forests admissible because there are adequate manufactured substitutes for timber – or is the extinction of a species of plant tolerable, if synthetic substitutes are available for its medicinal properties?

Even more widely, is it acceptable to trade-off roads, houses and factories for the environment? There is a range of conflicting answers to this question, each expressing different views about what is technically possible and what is thought to be ethically desirable for the environment (Table 3).

Table 3 Environmental viewpoints

Colour	Environmental viewpoint
Brown	All assets are substitutes. *Technocentric view:* benefits of technology and science embodied in people-made capital can outweigh the loss of natural capital stock. 'Technical fixes' can solve environmental difficulties. Unrestrained free markets are the best way of ensuring efficient use of resources. Unlimited growth not a problem.
Mid-green	Some substitution between natural and manufactured capital is possible but subject to the need to preserve essential natural resources – critical natural capital – in order to avoid irreversible environmental damage. Markets adjusted for 'market failure' – Green prices and standards. GDP growth constrained by the need to preserve a constant capital stock.
Deep green	Substitution undesirable. *Ecocentric view:* virtually all ecosystems should be conserved. Very deep green *bio-ethical* attitude: 'nature is sacred – all environmental assets (animate and inanimate) have moral importance'.

Colour	Environmental viewpoint
Deep green	Need for **steady-state economy**: zero GDP and population growth. Strong regulations rather than market forces to achieve environmental objectives.

Between 'brown' and 'deep green' there is a complete spectrum of overlapping shades of environmental opinion. Consequently a simple table cannot do justice to the complexity and subtlety of all views. However, a broad distinction can be made between two camps: the *anthropocentric* view – humankind at the centre of the world – which asks of the environment 'what value is it to us?'; and the deep ecology or *ecocentric* view – the non-human world has a valid claim to its existence quite apart from human needs. While the 'browns' are exclusively in the anthropocentric camp, green opinions straddle both the anthropocentric and various ecocentric viewpoints.

Bio-diversity

Conserving **bio-diversity** – the variety in all life forms – is also essential for the maintenance of a good-quality stock of natural assets. It is the destruction of habitats such as tropical forests, rather than over-exploitation, which is the main cause of the probable loss of one million species in the last 20 years, out of an estimated total of perhaps 30 million species. The case for bio-diversity is threefold:

- Wild species of plants and other life forms supply a significant amount of bio-chemical information from which modern medicines are developed. Approximately a quarter of prescribed medicines originate from plants. The familiar aspirin, for example, is based on a derivative of willow bark. Plants also provide material for breeding sturdier agricultural crops. Since future needs cannot be anticipated, a strong claim can be made for the greatest possible bio-diversity.

- The more abundant the bio-diversity, the greater the ability of the environment to withstand stress and shocks, such as floods, persistent drought or viral outbreaks. With a diverse genetic stock, there is a better possibility of adaption and the survival of environmental systems.

- Irrespective of its practical value, the diversity of life is important for the enrichment of human experience, as a source of wonderment, contemplation and questioning.

Maintaining bio-diversity is not without cost. It may be impossible to preserve all species and have development, but as the environmental economist Pearce has concluded:

'We should only degrade or deplete our natural capital stock – particularly resources that may be irreversibly lost – if the benefits of doing so are very large.'

'Mind if I smoke?'

Such important decisions require cost–benefit analysis, which is the systematic comparison of all costs and benefits, including externalities, extending into the foreseeable future (see Chapter 6).

Attitudes

Lester Brown, head of the Worldwatch Institution and a significant contributor to the Bruntland Report, has argued that the transition to a sustainable society requires not just a change in the way we manage our resources, but also a change in attitudes from the 'me now' concern of conventional economics to the consideration of 'others now and later'. The changes needed can be seen by comparing the dominant values of a sustainable society with those of our more familiar unsustainable society.

Most environmental economists agree with Brown about the importance of changing attitudes, although there is less agreement about how this might be achieved and exactly which values should be adopted.

- On the one hand there is the view that free markets, with their emphasis on the satisfaction of individual wants, undermine support for the wider community values essential for a sustainable environment.

- The counter argument is that markets can be a powerful way of expressing and ensuring green values. 'Green consumerism' has been successful in persuading many manufacturers to adapt their products to match the demands of a growing environmentally aware population. The 'deep greens', however, would claim that consumer preferences – for example, for unleaded rather than leaded petrol – are irrelevant because there should be fewer cars on the roads. The aim should be to reduce rather than change personal consumption.

BASIC ARGUMENTS OF THE PEARCE REPORT

1. Sustainable development is a necessary condition for survival.

2. Sustainable development entails adjusting economic activity so as to sustain the world's life support capacity. This implies:
   (a) maintaining the integrity of natural and semi-natural eco-systems
   (b) ensuring that the harvesting of timber and fish stocks takes place at sustainable yields
   (c) ensuring that discharges of waste occur at rates that are within the assimulative capacity of receiving environments
   (d) exploiting non-renewable resources at rates constrained by the development of replacement technologies so that future productive capacity is not reduced by current resource depletion.

3. A necessary condition for sustainable development is the correction for these sources of market failure. For this to be achieved the environment must be valued and environmental values incorporated into decision-making structures.

4. For private producers and consumers this means that the set of prices they face in the marketplace must be adjusted for environmental effects.

5. In the public sector, environmental values must be incorporated into decision-making structures. This can be achieved in three ways:
   (a) by extending the use of cost–benefit analysis to all public investment decisions
   (b) by introducing environmental conservation constraints into public investment programmes
   (c) by constructing national accounts to ensure that natural resource losses and gains are incorporated into measures of gross domestic product (GDP).

Source: Bowers (Banc)

Whatever views are finally espoused, the shift in attitudes is likely to come about by a combination of information, education, green consumerism and government action. The role of green pressure groups will remain central in increasing public awareness.

British policy on sustainable development

In the UK the concept of sustainable development was popularized in 1989 by the publication of *Blueprint for a Green Economy* (the Pearce Report), which was originally prepared as advice for the Department of the Environment (see the boxed item on page 46).

Many of these views – although some critics would say not enough - were reflected in the British government's first major statement on the environment, *This Common Inheritance* published in 1990. In this White Paper the government announced its acceptance of the concept of sustainable development which it interpreted as *'living on the earth's income rather than eroding its capital'*. By this, the government meant *'keeping the consumption of renewable natural resources within the limits of their replenishment and handing down to successive generations not only* [manufactured] *wealth but also natural wealth'*.

A more detailed statement of these principles, together with a policy plan, appeared in the Government's 1999 publication 'Sustainable Development: The UK Strategy'. This emphasized that the effectiveness of Government action depends upon *'developing a fruitful partnership between all the different sections of society'* and stressed that the *'choices and behaviour of individuals in their homes and working lives are perhaps the most significant of all.'* The translation of the UK Strategy into action is reviewed in Chapter 7.

International policy on sustainable development

The most significant event in the promotion of sustainable development was the United Nations' conference on Environment and Development – the 'Earth Summit' – held in Rio de Janeiro, Brazil, in 1992. At this meeting world leaders committed themselves to the principles of sustainable development when they agreed to *Agenda 21,* an environmental action plan for the next century. They also signed treaties on climate change and bio-diversity; agreed a statement of principles on forestry; and established a Sustainable Development Commission to develop and monitor progress on the implementation of Agenda 21 (see the boxed item). It can be seen that the Rio declaration echoes many of the themes raised in the Bruntland and Pearce reports, but will these ringing declarations really make any difference?

THE RIO DECLARATION

This declaration, about balancing the need to protect our environment with the need for development, is based on the following principles:

1. Sustainable development – because we are concerned about people's quality of life.
2. The sovereignty of states and their responsibility not to cause environmental damage beyond their frontiers.
3. The importance of development so as to meet the needs of present and future generations.
4. The importance of tackling poverty, one of the root causes of environmental degradation.
5. Reduction and elimination of unsustainable patterns of production and consumption.
6. Public participation in decision-making and access to information.
7. Preventative measures to protect the environment in the absence of full scientific certainty.
8. Application of the polluter pays principle by including environmental costs in the prices of goods and services.
9. Assessing the environmental impact of major projects.

The UN Conference on Environment and Development, popularly known as 'Earth Summit II', was held in New York in June 1997. This meeting was attended by representatives from 185 countries including 85 heads of state. Many delegates drew attention to the slow progress since Rio, and to the inconsistent fulfilment of agreements and weaknesses in enforcement procedures.

Critics have argued that the Earth Summits have produced few

MAIN POINTS OF THE KYOTO PROTOCOL

- Gases subject to mandatory cuts: carbon dioxide, methane, nitrous oxide, hydrofluorocarbons (HFCs)
- A total of 38 industrial countries agreed to legally binding targets for cutting their aggregate emissions of six gases by 5.2 per cent from 1990 levels between 2008 and 2012
- Russia, Ukraine and developing countries to be exempt from the new commitments
- Countries to be permitted to trade *emission quotas*
- Sanctions for countries which failed to reach their targets to be agreed at a later date.

---

binding agreements and only modest financial commitment. Although in the short run this is true, the two summits have helped to put the environment firmly on the agenda of international conference tables and set in motion changes that will gather momentum. Several legally binding treaties, with exemptions, have been agreed and more will follow – for example, the Kyoto climate conference in the December following Earth Summit II (see boxed item on page 48).

Concluding comment

At the core of the idea of sustainable development is the role of the present generation acting as a custodian for a stock of assets which is to be passed on to future generations. As Lester Brown has commented in his book *Building a Sustainable Society*:

> 'We have not inherited the Earth from our fathers, we are borrowing it from our children.'

To help us decide what to preserve and enhance, we need to develop ways of valuing natural assets – i.e. atmosphere, oceans – which are not normally priced in the marketplace. The Pearce Report has drawn attention to the necessity of an appropriate system of national accounts which shows depreciation of natural assets. These and other issues of environmental evaluation are considered in the next chapter.

KEY WORDS

Misallocation of resources	Intra-generational equity
Sustainable development	Inter-generational equity
Economic growth	Steady-state economy
Development	

Reading list

Bamford, C., Chapter 7 in *Transport Economics*, 2nd edn, Heinemann Educational, 1998.
Common, M., Chapter 9 in *Environmental and Resource Economics*, 2nd edn, Longman, 1996.
Grant, S., Chapter 5 in *Economic Growth and Business Cycles*, Heinemann Educational, 1999.
The UK's Strategy for Sustainable Development, HMSO, 1994.

Useful website
UN Commission on Sustainable Development:
www.un.org/esa/sustdev/

Essay topics
1. (a) Explain what is meant by sustainable development. [10 marks]
   (b) Discuss how sustainable development could be achieved. [15 marks]
2. Discuss whether a county should aim for high growth. [25 marks]

Data response question
This task is based on a question set by the OCR board in 1998. Read the following article, which is adapted from the *Daily Telegraph* of 9 September 1996, and then answer the questions that follow:

Inside Thailand – new cars face ban to ease congestion

New cars are to be banned from Bangkok during the rush hour in the latest scheme to ease the Thai capital's notorious traffic congestion. Some commuters say they spend 25 per cent of their lives in traffic jams. The ban comes a year after the deputy prime minister, Thaksin Shinawatra, asserted that 'within six months' he could solve the traffic crisis that has blighted the lives of Bangkok's eight million residents. That deadline came and went with no perceptible improvement on the gridlocked streets.

Children still leave home before dawn to get to school on time; drivers can be spotted eating their breakfast as they inch their way through a mass of fumes that consist of a toxic combination of carbon monoxide, lead and dust. About the only mode of transport guaranteed to ensure punctuality is the motorcycle taxi service - the fear of being late to those brave enough to use them is replaced by more pressing concern about losing limbs as these taxis make their way between lines of cars and ancient battered buses, with only inches to spare.

The scheme to ban new cars during the rush hour is extraordinary and comes into force on 1 January 1997 when all new cars will be fitted with a new style of orange number plates. Predictably, the ban has provoked intense opposition from the Thai Chamber of Commerce who are concerned about its economic implication despite the fact that traffic congestion is already costing the country an estimated equivalent of £1.5 billion a year.

Previous ambitious attempts to alleviate traffic congestion have failed.

The boldest measure was to stagger banking hours in an attempt to get 180 000 cars off the streets in the morning rush hour. Instead, it extended the rush hour and created chaos in Thailand's banking system. Bangkok is one of the few capital cities without a proper public transport system – an underground railway has been on the drawing board since 1976, yet construction work has never started despite contracts being drawn up and start dates set. Unlike some of its South East Asian neighbours, Thailand has never seriously considered road pricing. Transport planners, economists and academics believe it should. With no obvious solutions in sight, the only certainty is that the young men who provide motor cycle taxi rides will continue to offer their unique form of white knuckle rides for some time!

1. (a) Define the term 'negative externality'.[2 marks]
   (b) Drawing upon the information provided, explain how negative externalities arise from traffic congestion in Bangkok. [3 marks]
2. (a) What is 'road pricing'. [2 marks]
   (b) Explain the circumstances in which road pricing would have a significant effect on traffic congestion in Bangkok. [3 marks]
   (c) How does a road pricing approach compare with the other solutions mentioned in the article. [4 marks]
3. 'Traffic congestion is already costing the country an estimated equivalent of £1.5 billion a year.' Explain briefly how this figure might have been calculated and discuss the implications of this estimate for the Thai economy. [6 marks]

Chapter Five

How much for the environment?

'An economist is a person who knows the price of everything and the value of nothing.' Adapted from Oscar Wilde

This chapter looks at two related questions which must be faced, in order to decide on the correct amount of resources needed to save and improve the environment:

- How much are natural assets and environmental quality worth?
- Can the environment be included in national and corporate accounts?

Valuing the environment

It is mistakenly thought that – as the quotation heading this chapter suggests – economists have a narrow view of life, being interested only in 'market prices'. In fact, establishing ways of valuing environmental goods for which markets are absent or incomplete is an important concern of modern economics. The following section briefly reviews the scope and limitations of the various techniques currently in use.

Physical damage valuation

If the physical effects of pollution are measurable – for example, damage to health, crops or buildings due to air pollution – then the costs of these impacts and the value of avoiding them might be calculated. In the case of health these costs would include medical bills and the value of output lost due to illness. Although useful, the technique has limitations. It ignores, in the case of health, the distress of illness and has an unacceptably restricted approach to the value of fitness and the quality of life. It is of no help in cases of environmental damage where the physical effects, such as loss of landscape or species, cannot be translated into costs using market prices.

Willingness to pay

An alternative to concentrating on the cost of damage is to find out how much people are willing to pay for environmental improvement or preservation. There are two ways of doing this:

1. Revealed preference

This is known as **revealed preference** because, even where markets for environmental goods do not exist, consumers may indirectly reveal how much they value them, through other actions or expenditures. For instance, demand curves for the enjoyment of the countryside might be constructed from the travel times and costs people incur to reach their destinations, which can be regarded as a price paid for access to the countryside.

The demand for clean air and quietness has been inferred from comparisons of the prices of similar houses in areas differing in noise levels or air pollution. On a house costing £50 000, for example, various studies estimate that in certain areas a 10 per cent decrease in air sulphur pollution might raise the price by £600 and a one-decibel decrease in traffic noise by £250.

2. Stated preference

Typically this group of techniques (**stated preference**) involves the use of carefully worded questionnaires to find out people's **willingness to pay** (WTP) for environmental improvement, or **willingness to accept** (WTA) compensation for an equivalent deterioration in the quality or quantity of environmental assets. Illustrations, models and videos may be used to help make the questionnaire more realistic.

In its most simple form a WTP question might ask: 'How much are you willing to contribute to save a public woodland near your home?' It might be expected that, for a particular environmental good, the value at which people are willing to buy (WTP) would be equal to the value at which they are willing to sell (WTA). Disconcertingly, WTA values are usually significantly higher. No single, totally persuasive explanation has been found. Among possible explanations is the difficulty of replacing environmental goods with other goods. Stereos and mountain bikes, for example, are probably inadequate substitutes for the loss of woodlands. Higher compensation is required for the environmental loss.

A feature of some stated-preference techniques is the use of experimental designs, to construct a series of hypothetical alternatives from which individuals are then asked to choose. Instead of the question 'How much are you willing to contribute to saving the elephant?', respondents might be asked to rank, in order of preference, alternative wildlife programmes for a given cost, with different levels of preservation in the numbers of elephants, rhinos and mountain gorillas.

This technique can be extended to include manufactured as well as environmental assets. For example, in determining priorities for a development plan a local government council may have to consider:

- providing more industrial jobs
- preventing the loss of open land
- providing new housing
- conservation of wildlife
- promoting tourism in the area.

Data would be presented in the questionnaire, on the opportunity cost of, for example, extra houses or jobs in terms of the loss of open land or wildlife. Residents would then be asked to rank alternative development plans. This technique therefore provides information on peoples' marginal rates of substitution or trade-off between different goods or qualities of goods. If monetary costs can be put on one of the goods in the survey, then WTP can be estimated.

An obvious difficulty is that all the stated-preference methods rely on answers to hypothetical questions and may be subject to certain biases because respondents are not making real transactions.

'Hello! We can't be far from civilization'

Total economic value (TEV)

People may be ready to pay for environmental assets they never experience directly. Contributions to saving the panda, for example, or other threatened species, may come from people who never expect to see the creatures in the wild except in television programmes or photographs.

- **Use value** is what people are willing to pay to use the environment – for recreation; as a source of agricultural land and materials; as a receptacle for waste.
- **Option value** is the amount people are prepared to pay in order to

preserve the option to use some environmental asset at a later date. Even if the option is not exercised, the possibility of doing so may be a source of satisfaction.

- **Existence value** is what people will pay for the satisfaction of knowing that a species or habitat exists, although they will never visit or use it. Preserving the environment for one's heirs and for future generations, as well as a belief in the 'sanctity of nature', are among the sources of existence value.

Total economic value
= use value + option value + existence value.

National accounts

A precondition for the management of environmental resources is a comprehensive system of measuring the stock and use of such resources.

We might expect that a likely source for such information would be the official national accounts which measure, for each country, wealth in terms of the total value of the flows of output, income and expenditure – the gross domestic product (GDP). In fact conventional GDP accounts are a very poor measure of human interaction with the environment. This is because GDP figures capture only market and other recorded transactions (on page 16, Figure 3; the upper loop in the diagram), whereas for the environment (on the lower part of the diagram), markets don't exist or are incomplete.

Specifically, GDP figures fail environmentally for the following three reasons:

- They don't show the depletion of natural resources. A country that runs down its stocks of machinery, by failing to replace them as they wear out, will be shown to be poorer, but a country depleting its fisheries or forests appears in GDP accounts to be richer.
- No account is shown of the value of environmental changes on the quality of life – variations in air and water purity; noise, pleasant views, access to countryside.
- Although the benefits of environmental improvements don't figure in national accounts, regrettable or 'defensive' environmental expenditures such as the £8 billion clear-up bill for the Exxon tanker oil spill, for example, may paradoxically show as an increase in GDP.

Why not simply produce an environmentally adjusted 'green GDP' figure, equivalent to *total economic value* described in the last section?

An invaluable environment

Statisticians are trying to adjust measures of national wealth for pollution and depleted resources. This turns out to be all but impossible.

The answer might be obvious: adjust national accounts to take account of changes in the environment. Statisticians have laboured for more than a decade to find a way to do this. In 1993 the United Nations, whose System of National Accounts provides a standardized basis for countries to record changes in their income, expenditure and wealth, publish guidelines for 'satellite' – or separate – accounts that try to integrate environmental and economic measures. Many environmentalists want to go further and estimate a single measure of the effect of environmental damage on economic growth. This goal of constructing a 'green GDP' is an imaginative one. But increasingly, statisticians are concluding that it is unattainable.

Some assets, such as timber, may have a market value, but that value does not encompass the trees' role in harbouring rare beetles, say, or their sheer beauty. Methods for valuing such benefits are controversial. To get round these problems, the UN guidelines suggest measuring the cost of environmental damage. But some kinds of damage, such as extinction, are beyond costing, and others are hard to estimate.

Putting environmental concepts into economic terms raises other difficulties as well. Geography weighs differently: a tonne of sulphur dioxide emitted in a big city may cause more harm than the same tonne emitted in a rural area while a dollar's-worth of output counts the same wherever it is produced. And the exploitation of natural resources may not always have a cost. Is a country depleting resources if it mines a tonne of coal? All other things equal, the mining of that tonne might raise the value of the coal that remains in the ground, leaving the value of coal assets unchanged.

Some statisticians, such as Anne Harrison of the OECD, would like a compromise which at least tries to attach monetary values to the depletion of natural resources, while admitting that degradation may be almost impossible to capture. Statisticians, say this school, should continue to try to value whatever they reasonably can: but they may have to accept that degradation (such as the loss of clean air or nice views) cannot be included in national accounts.

The Economist, 18 April 1998

Experts are divided on this issue. Some favour measuring environmental impacts in monetary terms. Others support physical measures, such as the amount of sulphur dioxide and other pollutants emitted by each sector of the economy. The article 'An invaluable environment' from *The Economist* reviews some of the problems with these differing views, but emphasizes that a single satisfactory green measure of GDP is unlikely. However, the attempt to include the environment in our accounts should not be abandoned. To have some environmental measures is better than having no measures at all.

This is particularly important for reaching correct decisions on specific projects if they are to be environmentally sustainable – enlarging a motorway, building a dam or out of town shopping mall, for example. Each of these requires a careful balancing of all costs and benefits including environmental and other externalities. This process – *cost–benefit analysis* – is the theme of the next chapter.

KEY WORDS

Revealed preference	Use value
Stated preference	Option value
Willingness to pay	Existence value
Willingness to accept	Total economic value

Reading list

Beardshaw, J., Brewster, D., Cormack, P. and Ross, A., Chapter 46 in *Economics: A Student's Guide*, 4th edn, Addison-Wesley Longman, 1998.

Grant, S., Chapter 4 in *Economic Growth and Business Cycles*, Heinemann Educational, 1999.

Mankiw, N., Chapter 22 in *Principles of Economics*, Dryden Press, 1997.

Perman, R., Common, M., McGilvray, J. and Ma, Y., Chapters 10 and 12 in *Natural Resources and Environmental Economics*, Longman, 1999.

Resources and Environmental Economics, Longman, 1999.

Useful website

Office for National Statistics: www.ons.gov.uk/ons

Essay topics

1. (a) Explain how you would attempt to measure the extent to which living standards of citizens of different countries vary. [2 marks]
   (b) Discuss the difficulties which are likely to be encountered in attempting to construct and interpret such indicators to obtain an accurate reflection of differences in living standards. [6 marks]
   [Associated Examining Board, 1998]
2. Discuss whether the goods and services which create externalities should be necessarily be provided by government. [6 marks]

Data response question

This task is based on a question in a 1994 syllabus specimen paper from the University of Cambridge Local Examinations Syndicate. Read the article which features Allied Carbides plc, and then answer the questions.

Market distortion leading to pollution

Allied Carbides plc, which is located in Huddersfield, West Yorkshire, is a major producer of carbon black, an essential ingredient used in the manufacture of tyres and similar rubber products. The company has a 70 per cent market share in the United Kingdom, the remaining 30 per cent of manufacturers' needs being supplied from imports. Allied Carbides has expanded its operations in line with increased demand over the 42 years that it has been based on its present site. The company now employs 180 workers, mostly in the manufacture of carbon black. It is located in an industrial area of the town but as its manufacturing site has expanded then so it has become increasingly in conflict with residents of a nearby housing estate who have complained strongly about the detrimental effects that the company's operations are having upon the quality of their lives and upon the local environment.

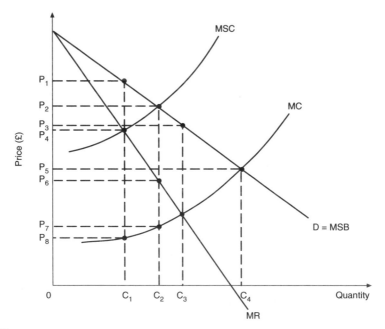

According to economic theory, the firm is producing in a situation where the market mechanism has failed to achieve the best allocation of resources due to:

- the problem of externalities
- its monopoly power

These market distortions can be illustrated by the diagram on the previous page which is taken from a recent economics textbook (J. Sloman and M. Sutcliffe, *Economics Workbook,* Prentice Hall, 1991). There is no easy solution to the problem faced by the residents on the one hand and Allied Carbides on the other hand. An interesting new approach, put forward by economists, focuses on the idea of 'pollution rights', details of which are outlined below in an extract from a recent article on this topic.

The traditional way of regulating pollution in the United Kingdom is by means of the *direct regulation* of industry, for instance by rules governing levels of pollution emission. The aim of measures such as the Clean Air Act and Alkaline Laws is to shift production methods towards those which make the optimum use of all resources, including environmental resources. Contrary to popular belief though, regulation does not eliminate pollution – it simply lays down minimum standards and as such, is unlikely to be as efficient as a *pollution charge or tax.* Taxation has various merits as a means of pollution control, although there are major practical difficulties to be overcome if so-called green taxes are to be accepted. In addition, it should be clearly stated that pollution taxes are relatively uncommon due to the political issues involved in their implementation. One particular concern is that the use of taxes in this way would be inflationary, although some would argue that this is a modest cost to pay for a more equitable and effective means of pollution control than direct regulation.

1. Why is Allied Carbides a monopolist? Analyse how you would expect it to operate relative to a firm in a more competitive market structure. [5 marks]
2. The following questions relate to the figure:
   (a) What is the firm's profit-maximizing price and output? Explain your answer. [2 marks]
   (b) What is the socially optimum price and output? Explain your answer. [2 marks]
   (c) If a pollution tax were imposed equal to the marginal pollution cost, what would be the level of the tax rate? [1 mark]

(d) Given that the firm is a monopolist, what would be the new price and output resulting from the imposition of this pollution tax? [1 mark]

(e) Would this be socially efficient? Explain your answer. [4 marks]

3. (a) Explain why 'taxation has various merits as a means of pollution control'. [7 marks]

(b) Why are pollution taxes inflationary? Discuss other likely economic drawbacks which might arise if pollution taxes were introduced in the United Kingdom. [8 marks]

4. The residents are pressing for Allied Carbides to relocate from their present site to one where they will be well away from people. Allied Carbides are not in favour of the move. As an economist, you have been asked to carry out a 'cost–benefit analysis' of this situation. Briefly describe the information you might need and how you could use it to arrive at an appropriate outcome. [20 marks]

Chapter Six
Cost–benefit analysis

'... *cost–benefit analysis is an imperfect calculus, as much an art as a science or, more precisely, as much a matter of judgement as technique.*'
E. J. Mishan

Introduction

In an economy with a well-functioning market, resources are allocated to their most highly valued uses via prices which reflect their relative scarcity. However, in the case of natural resources and environmental goods these markets frequently do not exist or, if they do exist, are distorted or malfunction in various ways. This *market failure* has its origins in such elements as externalities, unpriced assets, public goods, transaction costs and non-existent property rights. The most significant consequence of this market failure is a divergence between social and private costs and benefits.

Cost–benefit analysis (CBA) was developed by public sector economists in order to identify and quantify the social costs and benefits of public sector investment projects. Subsequently CBA was used to evaluate policies as well as projects. Whether used to evaluate projects or policies, CBA is essentially a decision-making tool which assesses the allocation of particular resources according to a comparison of the wider costs and benefits. If a proposal indicates that benefits will exceed costs then it can be approved, and where there are several proposals they can be ranked according to size of the total net benefit.

The development of CBA

Although the first recorded use of CBA was in France in 1840 when a civil engineer, Jules Dupuit, used it to estimate the benefits of a bridge, modern-day CBA has its origins in the USA where the Flood Control Act of 1936 stipulated that flood control projects should only be undertaken if 'the benefits, to whomsoever they may accrue' exceed the costs. By the 1960s CBA was being used to evaluate many aspects of the federal budget, including military expenditure, and by the 1970s its use had been extended to environmental and energy issues.

Two of the earliest examples of the use of CBA in the United

Kingdom are the evaluation of the M1 motorway in 1961 and the Victoria Line of the London Underground in 1963. A well known example is the 1967 Department of Transport investigation into the Cumbrian Coast railway line, but a significant one nevertheless because it represents an evaluation of disinvestment (i.e. closure) rather than investment. CBA was also used in 1970 by the Roskill Commission in its enquiry into the siting of a third London airport and by the Department of Energy in its 1981 and 1986 feasibility studies of a barrage across the Severn Estuary. For a recent example of CBA in the UK, see the 1996 investigation by the Home Office into road speed cameras (available at www.homeoffice.gov.uk/prgpubs/fprs20.pdf).

CBA procedure

In 1984, HM Treasury issued a set of guidelines to be used by government departments when undertaking investment appraisal exercises (CBA). The following procedure was suggested:

1. Define investment criteria
2. Identify options
3. Enumerate and calculate both direct and indirect costs and benefits of each option
4. Discount the monetary cost and benefits
5. Evaluate the risks and uncertainties
6. Consider the constraints
7. Present the conclusions indicating the preferred option and the basis of the calculation.

These guidelines represent a fairly standard approach to CBA and we can now discuss each in turn against the backdrop of current environmental concerns.

1. Define investment criteria

The most frequently cited investment criterion of CBA is the maximization of society's net benefit, and there are two classic positions on this topic.

Firstly, the **Pareto criterion** states that a net benefit exists when, following a change, at least one person is made better off without anyone being made worse off. Because of the very restrictive nature of this criterion – projects or policies involving income redistribution are clearly excluded – a second criterion known as the **Kaldor–Hicks criterion** is generally adopted. This approach, which forms the basis of current CBA, states that *a net benefit occurs when the sum of the benefits exceeds the sum of the costs, whether or not these benefits are* *used to compensate those who bear the costs.* That CBA does not address the issue of gainers compensating losers is clearly a major source of criticism to which we shall return.

Another investment criterion used in CBA and widely referred to in the literature is the maximization of the **benefit-cost ratio** (BCR). This states that only those projects whose BCR ratio exceeds 1 should be adopted. Where there are several alternative projects they are ranked according to their BCR ratio and the project with the largest ratio is chosen. Unfortunately these competing criteria can often provide contradictory outcomes, as Table 4 shows.

Table 4 Comparison of net present value (NPV) and benefit–cost ratio (BCR)

Project	Present value of costs (£)	Present value of benefits (£)	Present value of net benefits (£) (2/1)	Benefit– cost ratio (2–1)
A	100	350	250	3.5
B	300	600	300	2.0
C	350	900	550	2.6

The table shows clearly that if the benefit–cost ratio criterion is used then project A is the preferred option, but if the present value of net benefits criterion is used then project C is the preferred option and project A becomes the least preferred option. Theoretically net present value is the most satisfactory criterion but it has been argued that other criteria should be included, particularly where a choice has to be made between a cluster of projects of various sizes with different NPVs. In this situation it is claimed that the BCR ratio is more appropriate.

Current research by the United Nations Development Programme has focused on attempts to formulate an approach to CBA which is consistent with sustainable development. What is emerging is the idea that in the foreseeable future, projects will be ranked not by their net present values but by the new concept of sustainable net benefit which includes many of the ideas covered in Chapter 4. Such a criterion would have obvious implications for current CBA procedures.

2. Identify options
For any given investment project there are likely to be several different options available. For example, the Department of Environment,

A5 bypass plans axed to spare Snowdonia

The Welsh Office controversially axed two massive A5 bypass plans yesterday, to protect the rural beauty of North Wales.

For the first time, the Snowdonia countryside was given precedence over the drive for faster motor traffic and the Bethesda and Llangollen bypasses were axed.

The announcement was cheered by environmental, wildlife and countryside groups which had campaigned for years against turning the A5 into a Euroroute.

Bethesda bypass would have torn its way through local woodland and the proposal to straighten the Padog Bends would have created a three-lane highway through 20 acres of National Trust land.

The Daily Post, 12 March 1997

Transport and the Regions (DETR) have might allocated funds to solve the traffic problems of an historic town where congestion is causing long delays, accidents to pedestrians, pollution and damage to buildings. Planners identify three possible routes for the bypass:

- a northern bypass
- a southern bypass
- realignment and widening of the existing road.

Additional options might include delaying or phasing-in any of the above, taking policy measures rather than spending decisions and simply doing nothing. In some instances doing nothing, with its own costs and benefits, is quite a sensible decision and makes more sense than proceeding with a project which wastes resources. Doing nothing also provides a benchmark which can be used to judge the real impact of a project.

3. Enumerate and calculate costs and benefits

The principal distinction between the selection of projects in the private sector and the public sector is that the former is primarily concerned with private costs and benefits and their impact on profits, whereas the public sector, with its concerns for the welfare of society as a whole, needs to take account of the wider social costs and benefits arising from any particular public investment. Of particular concern are the externalities generated by a project, whether these are positive or negative. It is only when these have been identified and quantified that total social cost and benefits can be calculated.

(i) Real and pecuniary costs and benefits

The first step in the enumeration of the social costs and benefits of any project is to distinguish between real and pecuniary costs and benefits. Real benefits are those benefits which are enjoyed by the consumers of the public project and as such reflect the increase in society's welfare. Real costs are the opportunity costs involved in withdrawing resources from other uses. For example, if we consider the bypass proposal mentioned earlier, we can identify the reduction in travel time and the reduction in accidents as real benefits which accrue to the motorists using the bypass. However difficult it may be to calculate these benefits, they quite clearly need to be included in any comprehensive appraisal of the bypass. In contrast, there may be other identifiable benefits which, because they are merely pecuniary, need to be excluded. Pecuniary benefits arising from the bypass would include the increase in the profits of those business, such as garages, pubs, cafes, etc., resulting from the diverted traffic. Since these gains would be offset by the losses incurred by similar businesses in the town itself there is no net gain to society. (Pecuniary benefits are similar to the transfer payments encountered in national income analysis.) In addition, to the extent that the increase in the profits of businesses located on the bypass is a reflection of the increase in traffic generated by the bypass, the benefits of which will have already been included as real benefits, their inclusion would involve double counting.

(ii) Direct and indirect costs and benefits

Another distinction which needs to be made is between direct (primary) and indirect (secondary) costs and benefits. In the case of our bypass example, the direct costs would include such items as the purchase of land and the cost of labour and materials used in its construction. Indirect costs might include the double glazing of nearby houses affected by the noise of the traffic using the bypass. The direct benefits of the bypass would include those mentioned earlier, such as reductions in journey times and accidents; whilst indirect benefits would include a less noisy and polluted town and possibly even a cappuccino at a pavement cafe!

(iii) Cost and benefit – tangible and intangible

Real costs and benefits can also be tangible or intangible. Given perfect markets, the tangible costs and benefits of a project can be measured by the prices of the goods or services involved. However, if market imperfections exist then market prices are not accurate reflections of the social valuation of these goods and services, and shadow or accounting prices need to be used to adjust for the distortion in market prices. Although this is a complication, it is not unduly problematic. Problems do arise when intangible costs and benefits have to be calculated. By definition they cannot be measured by using market prices since they do not exist and yet it is precisely these intangibles which are so important in CBA. For example, the construction of the bypass mentioned earlier would provide a reduction in journey times and accidents, but although they are very clearly benefits they are, nevertheless, intangible and some method of attaching a monetary value to them needs to be adopted.

Taxes on motorists should be tripled to reflect the true cost of road transport, which adds £11 billion a year to health bills because of exhaust pollution, according to a report published by the British Lung Foundation in February 1998. Professor David Pearce, the author of the report, arrived at this figure by measuring the health effects and the willingness of people to pay to avoid the suffering caused by pollution.

(iv) Valuing time, noise and accidents

In valuing time a distinction needs to be made between working time and leisure time. The principle generally adopted in CBA for the valuation of working time is that one hour of working time saved is worth the hourly wage rate, whilst the valuation of leisure time is usually based upon the observed trade-offs which people make when confronted with the choice of a cheap but circuitous route and a more direct but expensive one. The monetary value of the reductions in accidents could be calculated by using existing DETR methodology, where the cost of road accidents is based upon the costs incurred by the NHS in treating road accident victims as well as the associated police and legal costs. The cost of the lost output of those injured should also be included. One estimate of the cost of road accidents is given in Table 5 (opposite).

Levels of noise in the environment would be significantly affected by the bypass. Lower noise levels in the bypassed town would be an obvious benefit to the townspeople, whilst people living adjacent to the new bypass would incur major costs because of the higher noise levels. The Eighteenth Report of the Royal Commission on Environmental Pollution – *Transport and the Environment* (Cm 2674), published in 1994, identified road traffic as the most common and most pervasive

Table 5 The cost of road accidents

Type of accident	Number of casualties	Cost per casualty	Total
Fatal	3 814	£744 060	£2.84 billion
Serious	45 009	£84 260	£3.79 billion
Slight	257 197	£6 540	£1.68 billion
			£8.31 billion

Source: Royal Commission on Environmental Pollution, *Eighteenth Report – Transport and the Environment*, Cm 2674, 1994

source of noise in the environment and estimated its overall cost at between 0.25 per cent, and 1.0 per cent of GDP. At a more personal level, the 1996 White Paper *Transport: The Way Forward* (Cm 3234) suggested that on average an individual would value a decrease in noise of one decibel at between £5 and £10 per annum. (A decrease in noise of ten decibels (dB) is perceived as a halving of noise so that the noise level in a house, 60 dBs, with a window open on to a busy road would be twice the received level of noise, 50 dBs, if the window were closed.)

(v) Atmospheric pollution
The construction of the bypass would also have an effect on atmospheric pollution in the area. Although pollution in the town itself would be abated in the immediate area of the bypass, it would increase and these effects would need to be quantified. The 1996 White Paper suggests that on average an individual would value a reduction in particulates by one microgram per cubic metre at between £5 and £20 per annum. This is the

Prescott blames Europe for failure to hit clean air target

The government has been forced to abandon ambitious plans to cut the amount of dust produced by diesel exhausts – but has blamed the embarrassing U-turn on pollution from Europe.

Mr Prescott admitted that airborne dust, which lodges in the lungs and hastens the death of more than 10 000 vulnerable people a year in Britain, is proving so difficult to prevent that reduction limits have been abandoned.

The Guardian, 14 January 1999

context of average UK levels of 10–15 micrograms per cubic metre in rural areas and 20–30 micrograms in urban areas.

Consider also carbon dioxide (CO_2) which is the most significant of the greenhouse gases implicated in global warming (which has its own costs and benefits). In the UK, some 24 per cent of total CO_2 emissions come from surface transport of which 87 per cent originates from road transport. The 1996 White Paper used the average cost to world GDP each year of global warming over the period to 2050 as the basis for estimating the cost of damage caused by CO_2 emissions. It estimated a cost of responsibility for UK transport at between £1.8 and £3.6 billion.

This discussion of CO_2 highlights the inside versus outside problem of CBA where a distinction needs to be made between benefits and costs which accrue inside the jurisdiction where the project is undertaken and those which occur outside. For example, in using CBA to evaluate the UK road building programme just how much importance would be attached to the costs of increase in CO_2 levels? Should they be included at all? In practice it is extremely difficult to draw a clear geographical boundary within which all costs and benefits occur and beyond which they do not, but a decision has to be made nevertheless.

Britain's plans to cut levels of two traffic-related air pollutants are being watered down. By 2005 concentrations of particles with a diameter of less than 10 micrometres were to be allowed to exceed 50 micrograms per cubic metre, averaged over 24 hours, only 4 times a year. This has been changed to 35 times a year. The 2005 target for hourly average nitrogen dioxide levels is also being relaxed, from 150 to 200 parts per billion.

New Scientist, 23 January 1999

Other intangibles would be the effect, positive or negative, which the construction of the bypass would have on the flora and fauna in the area. As we have seen already, such is the difficulty in quantifying these effects they are left out of the CBAs conducted by the DETR, but they are included in the environmental assessments to reflect growing public concern about the loss of habitat and the threat to bio-diversity.

(vi) Biased calculations

A problem which often emerges in CBA is **institutional capture**, where institutions and organizations use it for their own ends. For example, those who incur the costs of a project have a tendency to exaggerate them and to minimize the benefits, whilst those who have a vested interest in the project, such as construction companies or environmental groups, can be expected to minimize the costs and inflate the benefits. Although initially hostile to the whole concept of CBA, many environmentalists can now see the advantages of such an approach provided that the costs and benefits about which they are so concerned are included in the analysis.

Some of the environmental degradation perpetrated by the Tennessee Valley Authority and others is carried out through the sophistry of cost–benefit analysis. One example was the US Army Corps of Engineers' $15.3 million Gillham Dam across the Cossatot River in Arkansas, which was halted by an Environmental Defense Fund sponsored injunction against the Corps. Three-quarters of the benefits claimed for Gillham Dam, $970 000 annually, were in flood damage that the Corps said the dam would prevent. Yet on the 50 miles of the flood plain below the dam there was virtually nothing to protect – in sum, three old wooden bridges, a dozen summer homes, and about 20 miles of gravel road. There had never been a recorded flood death on the Cossatot.

Upon inspection it appears that the figure of $970 000 was arrived at by the Corps through some circuitous reasoning. The dam was expected to result in a considerable growth in population and industry, which would mean that new buildings would be built on the present flood plain. It was the value of these anticipated structures that was being protected from flood by the dam. The only real beneficiaries of the dam, it turned out, were landowners who would reap a windfall profit as their forests were converted to industrial parks.

---

4. Discount monetary costs and benefits

It is this stage in the CBA procedure which generates the most controversy among environmentalists and in order to understand the arguments involved we need to look at the rationale for a practice of discounting in some detail. In Chapter 3 we discussed the concept of *inter-temporal equity*, that is, fairness between generations. Comparing the value of money, resources or consumption over time, however, raises certain difficulties. The difficulties arise from the fact that most people have a preference for money or consumption today rather than at some time in the future. In other words they are attaching a different value to the same thing as it occurs over time. For example, if someone would prefer to have £100 now rather than the same £100 next year (which is usually the case), they are implicitly saying that the one £100 is more valuable than the other. There are three possible explanations for this:

- Firstly, people generally prefer to have things now rather than later, whether it is a sum of money, its equivalent in resources or even a good time! Economists describe this as pure time preference and apart from simple impatience – it has its source in the risk of death (people might not be alive at some time in the future) and as well as uncertainty – who knows what the future might hold? For example, some catastrophe might occur to prevent the consumption of something which could have been consumed today. And people's preferences themselves may change over time so that what is forgone now for the sake of future consumption may not even be wanted in the future.

- Secondly, a sum of money received now could be invested and, at a positive rate of interest, would be worth more in, say, a year's time than the same amount of money received a year hence. For example, £1000 received and invested today at 5 per cent annual interest would, in a year's time, become £1050. By postponing the receipt of the £1000 for one year this opportunity to earn interest of £50 is lost. There is, in other words, an opportunity cost involved. This explanation is more commonly referred to as the capital productivity rationale for present consumption over future consumption.

- Thirdly, we would normally expect incomes and living standards to increase over time, but the theory of diminishing marginal utility tells us that the value of an extra slice of income is less than the preceding slice of income. Thus, as individuals see their incomes increase over time each pound spent in the future buys less utility. It is therefore worth less than a pound today which can buy more utility.

These are the explanations for **personal time preference** and in a market economy where consumer sovereignty prevails and individual preference determines the allocation of resources, the conventional view is that time preference should be considered alongside all other preferences in the economic decision-making process. Since a society is a collection of individuals, all of whom have time preference, society must also have a time preference. In this case we refer to **social time preference** which, whilst positive, is generally regarded as being less strong than personal time preference.

The process by which individuals or society explicitly recognize their time preference by attaching a current value to a sum of money or

Table 6 Estimates of the environmental costs of road transport in Great Britain (£ billion per year at 1994 prices)

	Estimate 1	Estimate 2	Estimate 3
Air pollution	2.0–5.2	2.8–7.4	19.7
Climate change	1.5–3.1	0.4	0.1
Noise/vibration	1.0–4.6	0.6	2.6–3.1
Total environmental costs	4.6–12.9	3.8–8.4	22.4–22.9
Road accidents	5.4	4.5–7.5	2.9–9.4
Total social and environmental costs	10.0–18.3	8.3–15.9	25.3–32.3
Congestion costs	Not included	19.1	19.1
Total transport externalities	10.0–18.3	27.4–35.0	44.4–51.4

Source: Royal Commission on Environmental Pollution, *Twentieth Report – Transport and the Environment*, Cm 7752, 1996
Estimate 1: Royal Commission *Eighteenth Report*, 1994
Estimate 2: Newberry *Economic Journal 105*, 1995 *Estimate 3*: Maddison and Pearce *Blueprint 5: The True Cost of Road Transport*, 1996

environmental resource occurring in the future is known as **discounting**. Its use in the past in cost–benefit analysis has been relatively uncontroversial, but its application to environmental impact assessments has been questioned by many environmentalists and even some economists. Before we look at this controversy, however, let us spend just a little time doing some simple calculations.

The arithmetic of discounting
Discounting is simply the reverse of the more familiar process by which a sum of money invested at a positive rate of interest grows as it is carried into the future. For example, £82.19 invested at 4 per cent grows to £100 at the end of five years. Conversely, the present value of

Table 7 The effect of different discount rates

Income	Discounted at:		
	5%	10%	15%
£100 at end of year 1	£95.24	£90.90	£86.96
£100 at end of year 2	£90.70	£82.65	£75.76
£100 at end of year 3	£86.38	£75.19	£65.79
£100 at end of year 4	£82.27	£68.50	£57.14
£100 at end of year 5	£78.35	£62.11	£49.75
Total of present values	£432.94	£379.35	£335.40

£100 to be received five years from today when discounted at 4 per cent is only £82.19 (see Table 7 on the preceding page). Two conclusions are clear from Table 7. Firstly, that for each **discount rate** the present value of a sum of money shrinks the further that sum is from the present. Secondly, that for any given year, the higher the discount rate the smaller the present value of any sum of money.

Discounting formula
The present value of any series of future sums can be found by using the formula:

$$PV = \frac{S_1}{(1 + r)} + \frac{S_2}{(1 + r)^2} + \frac{S_3}{(1 + r)^3} \ldots \frac{S_n}{(1 + r)^n}$$

where
PV is the present value,
r is the discount rate
$S_1 \ldots S_n$ are the future sums.

For example, suppose an income stream of £200 per annum for five years discounted at 8 per cent :

$$PV = \frac{200}{(1+0.08)} + \frac{200}{(1+0.08)^2} + \frac{200}{(1+0.08)^3} + \frac{200}{(1+0.08)^4} + \frac{200}{(1+0.08)^5}$$

$$PV = \frac{200}{1.08} + \frac{200}{1.17} + \frac{200}{1.26} + \frac{200}{1.36} + \frac{200}{1.47}$$

$$= 185.18 + 170.94 + 158.73 + 147.0 + 136.0$$

$$= £797.85$$

Thus the £1000 accumulated at the end of five years has a *present value* of £797.85.

Had we been discounting over 25 years the present value would have been less than 10 per cent of the nominal value, and over 50 years it would have been less than 1 per cent of the nominal value. Such is the impact of discounting, and we can begin to see why some environmentalists question its use, encouraging, as it does, present over future consumption.

The choice of discount rate

The foregoing discussion has explained the rationale for discounting but it hasn't told us what the discount rate should be. Should it reflect personal time preferences or social time preference? If we are to respect consumers' preferences regarding individual items of consumption then logically we respect their preferences for present rather than future consumption. This reasoning suggests that the discount rate should be determined by personal time preference, but such a rate is difficult to establish in practice and could, in fact, be very high – as much as 26 per cent according to one estimate.

In contrast, it could be argued that since individuals underestimate the importance of future consumption and overestimate the importance of present consumption, the social rate of discount should be used. Furthermore, some would claim that individuals, as members of society, *should* care more about the future and be compelled to act accordingly by the adoption of the lower social rate of discount. In other words, future consumption should be treated as a merit good.

Among those who accept the need for discounting, the consensus is that it should be determined mainly by the *social opportunity cost of capital*. Thus the 8 per cent rate currently used by the National Audit Office in its evaluation of public sector investment reflects broadly the rate of return in the private sector. In the Roskill Commission report a rate of 10 per cent was used and significantly the rate used by the Forestry Commission is only 3 per cent which reflects, no doubt, concerns about the viability of an investment the returns on which are, typically, some 50 years in the future. The opportunity cost of capital also explains the 10 per cent discount rate used by the World Bank in deciding its lending programme to developing countries.

Some environmentalists have argued for zero or even negative discount rates. A zero rate would mean that £1 today is worth £1 in future, whilst a negative rate would value £1 in the future as worth more than £1 today. The final section in this chapter will consider the reasoning behind such arguments.

Discounting and the environment

Discounting has been criticized by many environmentalists and some economists for several reasons:

Future generations

We saw earlier that one justification for discounting is that since future generations are likely to be better off than the present generation, a given sum of money in the future will, because of diminishing marginal utility, have less value than today. However, whilst this may be true of money it is doubtful if the same can be said of the environment. Although future generations may be better off financially and materially, all the present indications are that they will have less 'environment' in the future as a consequence of resource depletion, pollution and loss of habitat and species. If this turns out to be the case then future generations will, as the theory of diminishing marginal utility goes into reverse, place a greater value on the environment than the present generation. Hence the argument for negative discount rates.

Time preference
The time preference justification for discounting, with its emphasis on risk and uncertainty, has also been challenged on several grounds:

- The risk of individual mortality and its influence on inter-temporal choice cannot be used to justify society's inter-temporal choices because society is 'immortal' and is not, therefore, under the same pressure as the individual to consume now rather than later.
- Future preferences for a whole range of consumer goods may well be uncertain as tastes change and new products are developed but preferences for the life-sustaining environmental services such as energy, food and water are likely to remain constant and certain and their discounting cannot, therefore, be warranted on grounds of uncertainty.
- Even where uncertainty does exist it may be the result of something other than futurity, in which case discounting, especially using a single rate, is inappropriate.

Productivity of capital
The productivity of capital argument in defence of discounting has been challenged by the environmental economist Jacobs, who asserts that because £100 invested today will grow at a compound rate, it is absurd to suppose that £100 worth of environment today will also grow at a compound rate. Jacobs says: '... biologists have yet to discover a relationship between interest rates and the expansion of the earth's surface'. Discounting for him is a form of discrimination against future generations.

Present and future gains
Some critics have questioned not the use of discounting itself but rather the use of high discount rates on the grounds that it sacrifices the future environment for present gains. However, as the economist Pearce points out, this is not always the case. For example, although high discount rates may cause cost burdens to be passed on to future generations, those

Genetic food findings 'biased'

Leading consumer and environmental groups yesterday accused a House of Lords select committee on genetically modified foods of being biased, muddled and inaccurate after publication of a report that strongly backed the controversial technology. ...

The peers accepted in their report that there could be significant environmental risks in the technology but said that these were outweighed by substantial future economic benefits to farmers, the food industry and consumers. ...

The report was welcomed by the life-science industry but a Friends of the Earth spokesperson said the committee had been bamboozled.

The Guardian, 22 January 1999

same discount rates, based on the social opportunity cost of capital, will discourage investment and slow down the very economic growth which causes so much harm to the environment. Similarly with natural resources, the demand for which varies inversely with the discount rate.

5. Evaluate the risks and uncertainties

Despite the growing sophistication of the measurement techniques used in CBA, decisions are, nevertheless, made in ignorance about the future. For example, assumptions have to be made about the physical quantities and qualities of inputs and outputs of the project; the future prices of these inputs and outputs; the life of the project; and the nature of consumer demand. Furthermore, predicting the environmental consequences of projects creates additional uncertainty. Thus the widespread use of DDT in the 1950s created major short-term benefits through the control of mosquitoes and crop pests, but its very harmful long-term consequences for bird populations were not anticipated. A more recent example is the concern about the uncertainties surrounding the use of genetically modified crops (see above).

In CBA, *uncertainty* is not the same as *risk*. Where it is possible to identify the probable outcome of a project the issue is one of risk, but where such probabilities cannot be estimated the issue becomes one of uncertainty. In other words, risk is measurable uncertainty, which means that within CBA a risky outcome is more easily handled than an uncertain one. Risk is incorporated into CBA by weighting each possible outcome by the probability of its occurrence. Uncertainty is rather more difficult to deal with and, although complex procedures have been developed to respond to it, a commonsense approach is to generate additional relevant information before decisions are made. If it cannot be demonstrated that some outcomes are more certain than others, then there are no rational grounds for taking a decision. Indeed, in many areas of environmental analysis further investigation into areas of uncertainty has produced significant gains.

An alternative and less ambitious method of dealing with projects where little is known about the outcomes or their probabilities is to conduct a *sensitivity analysis*. For example, a CBA of a nuclear power station might be conducted by taking a variable, say the price of oil, and assuming the most pessimistic value, the most optimistic value and a range of values in between. Sensitivity analysis is also used to examine the impact on projects of variations in the discount rate. Thus, for any given project a discount rate of say 5 per cent might produce benefits greater than costs whilst a 10 per cent discount rate might produce costs greater than benefits.

6. Consider the constraints

Although the maximization of society's net benefit is the primary aim of CBA, it is important to recognize that there are likely to be various constraints which make this difficult or impossible to achieve – so forcing decision-makers to adopt a less than optimum solution. The most important of these constraints are:

● Technology constraints – the possible alternatives under consideration may be limited by the existing production function and technology. For example, nuclear fusion offers virtually unlimited supplies of energy without the dangerous radioactive

---

The environmental movement has tended to be deeply distrustful of the decision-making process, not least where CBA is practised, on the grounds that government departments and agencies are able to manipulate supposedly impartial procedures to get the results they want. For example a study of CBAs for land drainage schemes in the UK (often involving considerable ecological damage) identified sixteen techniques by which assessments were biased in favour of drainage. Appraisal of trunk roads using the joint CBA and environmental impact assessment framework do not appear to have had any effect on the volume of road building at all.

Source: M. Jacobs, *The Green Economy*, 1991

---

waste associated with nuclear fission. Unfortunately, despite the billions of pounds spent on research, the technology does not yet exist to harness the energy created during nuclear fusion, so we have to work within existing technological constraints imposed by nuclear fission.

- Legal constraints – national and international law concerning such things as due process, planning procedures and property rights would impose limits on a particular agency's activities. Thus Directive 85/337/EEC of the European Union introduced a system of environmental impact assessments to be used by member states in the prior evaluation of the possible effects of public and private projects on the environment.

- Administrative constraints – the successful implementation of a project requires that sufficient competent personnel be available to carry it through. If the skilled staff are not available then even the best conceived project with a very high net present value (NPV) is worthless.

- Distributional constraints – the costs and benefits of a project are usually distributed unevenly. For example, the benefits from one project may accrue to a low income group whilst those of another project may accrue to a high income group. If other things are equal

£400 000 cost of saving newts

Councillors are outraged that a campaign by activists to save protected newts has cost the local authority £400 000.

'At a time when we have limited budgets to spend on vulnerable elderly people, children and people with disabilities, I am shocked that we have been forced to spend this amount of money,' said the chairwoman of Flintshire's social services committee.

The council's arms-length disposal company, AD Waste, is moving from the nearly full Standard tip in Buckley to former Brookhill Quarry also near Buckley. If the move does not go ahead the council would have to spend a lot of money transporting waste out of the county.

Greater crested newts – a legally protected species – were discovered in Brookhill and had to be moved to a specially built site for protection. But conservationists lodged a whole series of complaints, called the police and went to the European Commission, alleging that the council had not done the job properly.

Flintshire believes the extent of the works was far in excess of what was necessary to meet EU requirements. The authority says it was forced into the situation because it could have taken years to resolve in the courts.

The Daily Post, 3 February 1999

the first project may be preferred on distributional grounds. In addition, those groups who incur the costs associated with a project are invariably not the same as those who enjoy the benefits. In the case of the third airport for London, the Roskill Commission was criticized for not considering the distributional implications of a decision which would have created significant benefits for air travellers, typically those on high incomes, while those on low incomes would have borne the brunt of the costs in the form of higher noise levels.

- Political constraints – a project with the highest NPV may not be feasible because of the slowness of the political process. Public enquiries into nuclear facilities and major road schemes are typical examples of this. Strong pressure groups can also prevent the adoption of policies with the potential of large net benefits. The

---

Reviewing the role of cost–benefit analysis

It has long been recognized that rigorous appraisal of options, both in helping to decide which options should be taken forward and to determine relative priorities for investment, plays a vital role in shaping programmes of transport infrastructure improvement. Cost–benefit analysis (CBA) has traditionally formed the quantitative element of such appraisal, with benefits calculated in terms of journey time savings, accident reduction and lower vehicle operating costs. In the consultation paper we expressed our view that cost–benefit analysis continues to provide a sound starting point for the appraisal of transport problems but indicated that we would welcome comment on how the appraisal system might be improved and extended ...

There was a comparatively widely-held view that CBA was too narrowly focused on economic benefits, failing to take into account environmental and social costs and benefits. It was accepted that there were practical and ethical difficulties in attempting to place a monetary value on the environment, but the pursuit of a wide-ranging numerically based analysis was considered to be high priority. Although the quantification of environmental, heritage and other wider factors was problematic, it was worth noting that CBA itself, while apparently a sophisticated numerical tool, was based on large numbers of assumptions about both absolute values and their weighting.

Source: *Driving Wales Forward: A Strategic Review of the Welsh Trunks Roads Programme*, Welsh Office, 1998

---

present government's attempt at restricting the use of the private motor car is a case in point.

● Budgetary constraints – frequently the largest of the options under consideration offers the highest NPV, but because of the need to work within a limited budget a smaller project with a lower NPV has to be chosen.

● Ethical constraints – the notion, implicit in CBA, that monetary values can, and should be, attached to such things as wildlife, scenic views, peace and quiet and so on is rejected by many people on the grounds that they have intrinsic value which puts them beyond price. For CBA to influence decision-makers its assumptions and procedures need to be acceptable to the public.

7. Presentation of conclusions

Handled with care, cost–benefit analysis is potentially a rigorous and systematic approach to the evaluation of alternatives, which has two essential characteristics: consistency and explicitness. In presenting the results of the analysis, the cost–benefit practitioner has to show that the calculations and results are consistent with the stated assumptions and objectives of the project. The procedures and methodologies need to be explicitly stated together with any relevant constraints. If these conditions are met then the conclusion of the analysis can be presented to the decision-maker as follows: 'Given that your objective is the maximization of net present value then, subject to certain specified constraints, the preferred option to A is …'

Concluding comment

The issues raised in this chapter have shown that there will be many occasions when, on completion of a cost–benefit analysis of a large project with significant and long-term environmental effects, there will be sufficient reasons why intelligent and reasonable people will disagree on the desirability of the project concerned. These are strong grounds for rejecting the view that cost–benefit analysis is an economic technique which can be mechanically applied to produce the correct solution. Instead, they are a reminder that used properly and sensitively, CBA provides a framework within which society can analyse and evaluate in a consistent fashion all the many economic and environmental effects of public expenditure.

KEY WORDS

Pareto criterion	Personal time preference
Kaldor–Hicks criterion	Social time preference
Benefit–cost ratio	Discounting
Institutional capture	Discount rate

Reading list

Anderton, A., Unit 38 in *Economics*, 2nd edn, Causeway Press, 1995.

Common, M., Chapter 8 in *Environmental and Resource Economics*, 2nd edn, Longman, 1996.

Griffiths, A and Wall, S. (eds), Chapter 10 in *Applied Economics*, 7th edn., Longman, 1997

Hanley, N. and Splash, C., Chapters 5 and 6 in *Cost Benefit Analysis and the Environment*, Edward Elgar, 1993.

Useful websites

The following web pages give some valuable insights into the cost–benefit techniques currently being developed by the Department of the Environment, Transport and the Regions:

www.roads.detr.gov.uk/roadnetwork/heta/hetacoba.htm

www.roads.detr.gov.uk/roadsafety/rvs/hen1_9.htm

www.roads.detr.gov.uk/roadnetwork/heta/sactra98.htm

www.roads.detr.gov.uk/itwp/appraisal/understanding/index.htm

www.roads.detr.gov.uk/itwp/paper/index.htm

The following web pages give a detailed account of the appraisal of police speed cameras:

www.homeoffice.gov.uk/prgpubs/fprs20.pdf

Essay topics

1. Describe the major steps in a cost–benefit study.
2. Discuss the arguments for and against a special, low or even zero rate of discount for environmental projects.
3. (a) Explain how and why cost–benefit analysis is applied by central government to decide upon major new road schemes in the UK. [10 marks]

   (b) Comment upon the extent to which this approach is valid where some roads are being funded and operated by companies in the private sector. [10 marks] [OCR, Transport Economics Paper, March 1997]

4. (a) Explain the main features of cost–benefit analysis. [12 marks]
(b) The Government is considering building a new underground railway line. Discuss the advantages and problems associated with cost–benefit analyis to decide whether or not the project should be approved. [13 marks] [AEB, Paper 2, January 1998]

Data response question

The area depicted in the map below is a stretch of agricultural land, consisting mainly of grades 2 and 3, lying between towns A and B. Agricultural land is graded on a 1 to 5 scale – grade 1 is 'exceptionally fertile' and grade 5 is classified as 'wasteland'. To the north there is an area of grade 1 land – also a site of special scientific interest (SSSI). To the west is a rapidly expanding industrial area heavily involved in the export trade.

There is a growing population here, incomes are high, and many people take frequent holidays on the coast and take the car ferry to France for shopping expeditions. Large numbers of foreign tourists use the A666 as they leave the ferry and head for the West Country.

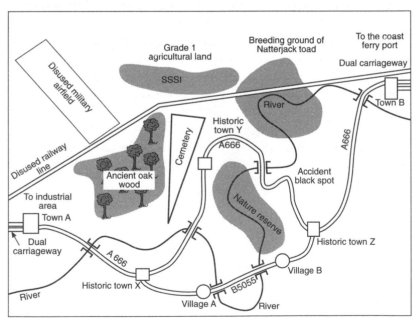

1. What are the transport problems in this area? [15 marks]
2. What environmental considerations would you need to take into

account in dealing with these problems? [25 marks]

3. How would you overcome the transport problems? [20 marks]

4. What economic cost–benefit concepts and procedures would you use in your analysis of the problems and decision-making? [30 marks]

5. Draw a map of your preferred solution(s). [10 marks]

Chapter Seven

Environmental improvement in theory: government action

'The primary virtue of the price mechanism is that it signals to con-sumers what the cost of producing a particular product is, and to pro-ducers what consumers' relative valuations are. In a nutshell this is the elegance and virtue of free markets which economists have found so attractive since the time of Adam Smith.'
D. Pearce, *Blueprint for a Green Economy*, 1989

Preliminaries

We have seen how environmental damage can be caused when markets do not work properly or because the necessary markets are missing. This and the following chapter review the theory underlying the repair work that can be carried out using the economist's toolkit of ideas and techniques. Chapter 9 then looks at the environmental policies that governments manage to deliver in practice.

First we shall review two broad categories of alternative remedies – private actions and government actions.

- Private actions rely entirely on individuals and organizations, unaided by governments, to sort things out. Possibilities here include:

  – Coase bargaining (see Chapter 3)
  – mergers between polluter and pollutee to internalize an externality
  – altruism: increasing green awareness may prompt firms and consumers to produce and buy environmentally friendly products.

- When private actions are inadequate, government intervention may be necessary. This can be a mix of command and control systems and **economic incentive systems.**

Using command and control (CAC) systems the government sets pollution standards or limits. These are enforced by inspection and backed by fines and criminal prosecution for transgression. Such systems simply replace market mechanisms. On the other hand, economic incentive (EI) systems aim to harness and improve, rather than supersede, market forces to achieve environmental ends. The following are some examples of EI systems:

- *Improving existing markets* with 'green' prices, corrected for the distorting effects of externalities by means of Pigouvian taxes or subsidies.
- *Creating new markets* by restricting the quantity of pollution, through the issue of a limited number of pollution permits that firms can trade between themselves. This internalizes the pollution externality by putting a price on it. Alternatively, congestion externalities (see Chapter 3), such as on motorways, can be internalized by pricing.
- *Market support* in, for example, the encouragement of the recycling of waste, by means of packaging taxes, recycling credits and disposal charges.

● Criteria
How do we decide which of the CAC and EI alternatives is the most effective? Taken from the influential book *Blueprint for a Green Economy,* the quotation which heads this chapter is enthusiastic about the virtues of markets, but in choosing between systems to combat environmental damage the following questions should be considered:

1. Cost
Is pollution being reduced in the most cost-effective manner? Does the anti-pollution strategy give incentives to find better and cheaper ways of achieving environmental quality? Environmental specialists describe this using the acronym **BATNEEC** – *best available technique not entailing excessive cost.*

2. Acceptability
Will the proposed solution command widespread acceptance in the community? This depends partly on whether it is regarded as equitable – not regressive in its income effects, and fair between polluter and pollutee.

The advantages and limitations of CAC and EI systems can be illustrated by comparing a 'green' or pollution tax with direct regulation in the form of an emission standard restricting the amount of pollution. Before we do this we need to make one more comment on variations.

● Types of taxes and standards
In the example we shall consider below, it is the quantity of pollution which is taxed – an **emissions** or **effluent tax**. This is the most effective tax because it deals directly with the source of the damage. However,

if the measurement of emissions is difficult or costly, then pollution may be taxed indirectly with an **input tax** placed on factors which contribute to the pollution – for example on unleaded petrol or fertilizers. Alternatively, outputs of the polluting manufacturer can be taxed – a **commodity** or **output tax**.

Instead of an emissions standard, the government may enforce a **technology standard**, insisting that firms use specific pollution-reducing equipment (e.g. gas filters on chemical refinery smoke stacks), or sell products that are designed to minimize pollution costs (e.g. cars with catalytic converters; aerosols without CFC propellants).

The impact of taxes and standards compared

In Figure 9, the socially efficient level of pollution is at 500 units, where the marginal social cost of pollution (MSCP) is equal to the marginal cost of abatement (MCA). An emissions tax of £2 per unit gives a powerful incentive for a firm to reduce its emissions from 750 to exactly 500 units, at which point MCA = £2. For any level of emissions above this it would be cheaper for the firm to reduce pollution to 500 units rather than to pay the tax because MCA is less than £2. For emissions reductions below 500 units the reverse is the case – the firm will pay an emissions tax of £1000 (500 × £2) and spend the amount indicated by the shaded area on clearing up pollution.

Compare this with an **emissions standard** of 500 units, vigorously enforced by inspection and fines, which appears to produce exactly the

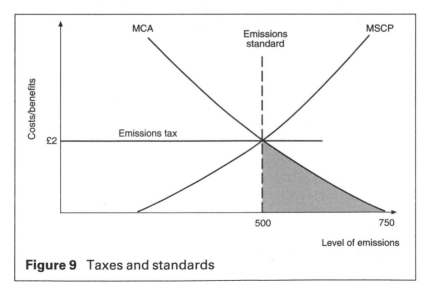

Figure 9 Taxes and standards

same socially efficient outcome. Is there nothing to choose between taxes and standards? Pollution taxes, it is claimed, are superior to standards in two respects.

● Costs

Imagine two firms, X and Y, each producing the same level of emissions, and sufficiently close to each other for the environmental damage created by each firm's factory chimneys to be the same. However, if the firms use different production processes, their clean-up or abatement bills for reducing pollution may differ. It may, for example, be more costly for firm X to reduce its emissions by 50 per cent than an equivalent reduction by firm Y.

This is shown in Figure 10, where the marginal cost of abatement curve for firm X (MCA_x) is above that of firm Y (MAC_Y). For the sake of clarity, this diagram does not include an MSCP curve as shown in Figure 9. Assume that it is estimated that the efficient level of pollution in this case requires total emissions from both firms together to be no greater than 10 units. As Figure 10 indicates, without any government intervention, X and Y would each pollute to a level 10 units, giving a total of 10 + 10 = 20 units.

Now suppose that the government wishes to reduce the total level of emissions from 20 units to the environmentally efficient level of 10

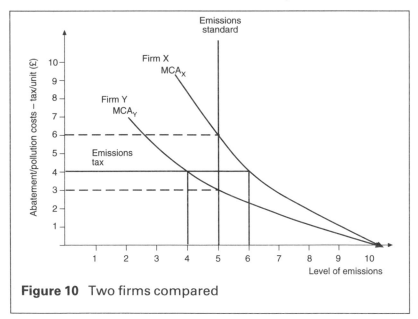

Figure 10 Two firms compared

units. It decides to achieve this by imposing an **emission standard**, restricting each firm's emissions to 5 units. This gives the target level of 10 units (5 units (firm x) + 5 units (firm y)) but is not the least costly way of reducing total emissions to 10 units. Figure 10 shows why. Recall that the total abatement cost of reducing emissions from one level to another is equal to the corresponding area under the MCA curve. If you are unsure about this, glance back at Figure 9, where the total cost of reducing emissions from 750 to 500 units is the shaded area below the curve. Thus in Figure 10, the total cost of reducing emissions from 20 to 10 units (a reduction from 10 units to 5 for both X and Y) is firm X's abatement costs – the area under MCA_x between 10 units and 5 units *plus* firm Y's abatement costs – the area under MCA_y between 10 units and 5 units.

As Figure 10 indicates, setting an emissions standard of 5 units for each firm is an unnecessarily expensive way of reaching the target of 10 units, because it breaks the **equi-marginal rule** for cost minimization. At the margin – reducing emissions from 6 to 5 units – the marginal abatement costs of the two firms should be equal. A comparison of the area in Figure 10 under MCA_x between 5 and 6 units, with the corresponding area under MCA_y shows that marginal abatement costs for firm X are substantially higher than for firm Y. At the very limit of the marginal unit, as each firm reaches the required emissions standard of 5 units, it can be seen that the marginal abatement cost of X is £6 and that of Y is £3.

If an emissions tax of £4 is introduced in place of a standard, each firm will decide to what extent it is cheaper to reduce emissions and avoid the tax, or to pay the tax. Firm X, with the higher abatement costs, will reduce pollution from 10 to only 6 units but firm Y, with lower abatement costs, from 10 units to 4 units. At this point the marginal abatement costs of both firms are £4 – equal to the tax – conforming to the equi-marginal principle necessary for efficiency. With the emissions tax there is a saving in the total cost of abatement. The £6 marginal cost of abatement from 6 to 5 units for firm X, necessary with a standard, is replaced, under the tax, with a £4 marginal cost reduction by firm Y. Again, if you are unsure about this simply compare, for the emissions standard and the emissions tax, the sum of the total areas under the relevant sections of the MCA curves.

• Incentives

With an emissions standard of 5 units, firm X has some incentive to adopt the superior technology of firm Y, moving to the lower MCA curve and reducing its costs by the shaded area. However, with the emissions tax the firm has an even greater incentive to reduce its abatemen cost, because it will also reduce its tax liability. *Thus, tax provides a constant spur for firms to adopt the most efficient abatement technology and so achieve the cleanest possible environment. This is in addition to the advantage, previously noted, of the incentive to reduce costs in accord with the equi-marginal principle.*

Does the polluter really pay?

A pollution tax is popularly thought to be fair because it seems to force producers, who are mistakenly regarded as the only source of pollution, to pay the tax – the PPP principle. What about consumers? It can be argued that they must also share some of the burden because they buy the goods which ultimately cause the pollution. *In fact, the expense of a pollution tax is likely to be divided between producers and consumers.*

Suppose pollution is handled by a *commodity tax* – in the form of a fixed tax per unit produced. Such a tax will probably see firms attempt to protect their profits, by charging a higher price and trying to pass the tax on to consumers (see Figure 11(a)). Although after tax the price which consumers pay, P_t, is higher than the original price P_0, they do not pay the full amount of the tax. Some of this is paid by producers, who now receive P_t minus tax per unit sold – less than the original price P_0.

Figures 11(a)–(c) show that the division of the pollution tax paid by producers and consumers depends, *with a given supply curve*, on the *price elasticity of demand*. The less price-elastic the demand curve, the greater the proportion of tax paid by consumers – Figure 11(b). The more price-elastic the curve, the more will be paid by producers – Figure 11(a). The incidence of tax is shared equally in Figure 11(c).

Although there will be some welfare losses from the tax – producers and consumers will buy and sell less than before – the net effect will be a gain for the community. The excessive pollution damage, previously unchecked because of externalities, is now at a socially efficient level. The tax-adjusted green price gives an accurate message to guide producers and consumers. If, for example, the demand for a good causing pollution is substantially price-elastic, then the green price will encourage consumers to switch to less damaging alternatives. The switch in demand from leaded to unleaded petrol, in response to a higher tax on the former, is a good example of this.

Pollution taxes are sometimes denounced because they seem to be harsh on poor people. The Institute of Fiscal Studies has, for example, calculated that a 15 per cent tax on domestic fuel in the UK would result

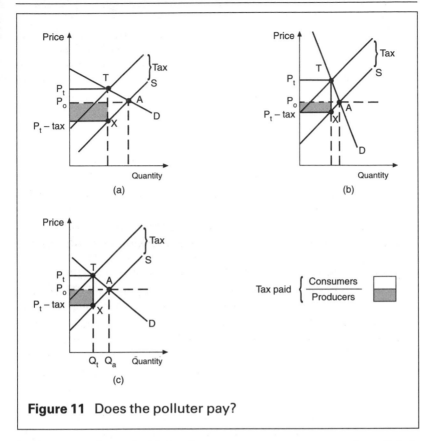

Figure 11 Does the polluter pay?

in the poorest households having to pay more as a proportion of their income (1.8 per cent) than the richest households (0.1 per cent) – an example of a *regressive tax*. However, the regressive effects can be reduced by targeting income supplements and tax concessions to the less well off. Moreover, the revenues from a pollution tax can be used by the government for grants to firms to encourage the development of products and processes that are environmentally less damaging.

Why standards?

We have shown that use of a pollution tax – a market-based system – has in theory considerable advantages over direct regulation of the command and control (CAC) type. Despite this, CAC systems, especially standards, are still the most widely used means of pollution control for the following reasons.

Popularity

- Standards, which appear to promise to reduce pollution to definite levels, are favoured by politicians and the public. They are simple to understand and have emotional appeal. Even if standards are sometimes inefficient and not always enforced, headlines proclaiming 'tough anti-pollution legislation' are more likely to win votes than taxes. To declare something illegal gives the impression that action has been taken.
- Standards are popular with administrators because less information is required for the introduction of the standards than with taxes. They also gain, in preference to taxes, grudging support from industry, especially from large firms who see possibilities for **regulatory capture** – persuading the pollution regulators to be sympathetic and 'reasonable' when setting and enforcing standards.
- A strong reason for preferring standards is the difficulty in obtaining satisfactory international agreements between governments on terms of pollution taxes. If pollution tax is imposed by one country alone it may put its producers at a disadvantage compared with overseas competitors. If consumers switch to purchasing imports, the level of pollution may not fall but its source will move abroad. However, it must be remembered that standards also create costs for an industry and international agreements on standards are equally desirable.

Safety thresholds

The vigorous enforcement of clearly defined standards may be the most suitable way of controlling highly concentrated, life-threatening pollutants – radioactive and certain chemical wastes – where it is essential that discharges are kept within tightly prescribed limits. In cases of this kind, safety rather than economy is clearly paramount. Nevertheless, for the bulk of pollution, the marginal damage curve rises only slowly. *In such circumstances market-based incentives, rather than standards, will produce a cleaner environment at lower cost.*

Markets in pollution rights

The advantages of market incentive systems can be combined with direct regulation by standards (refer back to Figure 10).

Assume, as before, two firms X and Y. The government sets an upper limit on total daily emissions of 10 units. Accordingly X and Y are issued with **pollution permits** allowing each of them 5 units of emissions. Since X and Y, without restriction, would each emit 10 units, a 5 unit per day abatement is required from each firm. The government allows the two firms to trade pollution permits between themselves for whatever price they can earn.

It will cost firm X, with the higher abatement curve, £6 to reduce its emissions from 6 units to the 5 units allowed by its permits. It would therefore gain, if instead of reducing its emissions to 5 units, it could buy an extra pollution permit for less than £6 allowing it to pollute up to 6 units. Firm Y, with a lower abatement cost, will find it profitable to reduce its pollution below 5 units, selling one of its pollution permits for more than £4 – its marginal cost of abatement from 5 to 4 units. Between £4 and £6, the pollution permits will be traded. Firm X will now emit 6 units and firm Y will emit 4 units.

Some critics mistakenly regard this exchange as unethical and call pollution permits 'cancer bonds'. The market in pollution permits has simply internalized and priced an externality. Consequently, the target of a total of 10 units of pollution from X and Y has been achieved in the most cost-effective manner, in accordance with the equi-marginal principle. Firm Y, with lower abatement costs, makes the largest contribution reduction.

The creation of markets in pollution permits has been pioneered in the USA. In May 1992, for example, under the 1990 Clean Air Act, the Tennessee Valley Authority (TVA) bought an estimated £2.5 million worth of credits from Wisconsin Power and Light, which fell below its allowable limit of sulphur dioxide emissions. This transaction has been criticized for allowing further pollution in an already polluted area.

The success of markets in transferable permits will depend on many things, including: the initial allocation of permits; the competitiveness of the market; and the effectiveness of the agency running the scheme. However, such markets, properly organized, do offer the possibility of cost-effective ways of reducing pollution. They may also be more welcome to industry than pollution taxes. The growing international acceptance of this idea was seen at the Kyoto conference (see page 48) where environmental targets were linked with a system of internationally tradeable permits or budgets.

KEY WORDS

Economic incentive systems	Technology standard
BATNEEC	Emissions standard
Emissions/effluent tax	Equi-marginal rule
Input tax	Regulatory capture
Commodity/output tax	Pollution permits

Reading list

Davies, B., Hale, G., Smith, C. and Tiller, H., Chapter 3.18 in *Investigating Economics*, Macmillan, 1996.

Grant, S., Chapter 25 in *Stanlake's Introductory Economics*, Longman, 1999.

Griffiths, A. and Wall, S. (eds), Chapter 10 in *Applied Economics*, 7th edn, Longman, 1997.

Hare, P. and Simpson, L., Chapter 12 in *British Economic Policy*, Harvester Wheatsheaf, 1993.

Useful websites

UK Environmental Protection Agency: www.environment-agency.gov.uk/

DETR: www.roads.detr.gov.uk/itwp/paper/index.htm

Essay topics

1. (a) Explain why economists regard pollution as an example of market failure. [10 marks]
   (b) How might pollution problems be dealt with through taxation? Comment upon how this approach compares with that of using legislation to control pollution. [15 marks] [OCR board 1997]
2. (a) Distinguish between private and social benefits. [10 marks]
   (b) Evaluate the policy measures a government could adopt to increase the use of public transport. [15 marks]

Data response question

This task is based on a question set by the OCR board in 1997. Read the article and then answer the questions that follow.

Cavalier Pet Products

Cavalier Pet Products is a large privately owned manufacturer of canned pet foods based in Bolton, Lancashire. The company, which employs 300 people, is long established and has been on its present site since it was founded by its owners, the Fazackerley family, in 1906. It is a market leader, producing own-branded products that are widely advertised and well known.

Through the nature of its manufacturing processes, the company is a polluter of the local environment. The nauseating smells from the factory, particularly in hot weather, are the main source of complaint; the firm also creates noise disturbance and quite recently was successfully prosecuted for discharging effluent into a local stream running alongside the factory. There is increasing local pressure from residents for something to be done about the whole question of the firm and its operations.

The obvious answer is for the firm to move to another location. The managing director of Cavalier Pet Products, Basil Fazackerley, favours such a move but is quite adamant that 'we shall not pay the full cost. If the local council want us to move, then they will have to help us to do so.'

The decision to relocate the factory has long-term implications both for its owners and for the community. In particular, new jobs will be created as the firm increases output and the local environment within the vicinity of the present site will experience environmental gain.

The local authority have agreed to contribute to the relocation, as they can see a benefit to the community. Cavalier Pet Products remains concerned that it should pay a realistic contribution to the cost of relocation.

In order to sort out these difficulties, a local university was asked to carry out a cost–benefit analysis of the proposed relocation. A summary of their findings is given in the table.

Table A Estimated discounted costs and benefits of the relocation of Cavalier Pet Products (£000)

Costs		Benefits	
Private costs of the relocation	1300	Private benefits	1500
Contribution from local authority	300	External benefits	1200
External costs	400		
Total costs	2000	Total benefits	2700

1. (a) State briefly what is meant by a 'negative externality' and give *two* examples of negative externalities arising from the firm's operations at its *present* site. [6 marks]
   (b) Examine the consequences of these negative externalities for (i) the firm, (ii) consumers of the firm's products, and (iii) local residents. [9 marks]
2. Excluding relocation, explain what other methods might be proposed by economists in order to deal with the problems arising from the firm's operations. [10 marks]
3. (a) Use the information provided to demonstrate how cost–benefit analysis is taking a long view and a wide view of this project. [2 marks]
   (b) What is the specific purpose of cost–benefit analysis in this case? [2 marks]

(c) With reference to the proposed relocation, give an example of (i) a private benefit, and (ii) an external benefit, arising from the proposed relocation. Justify your choices. [6 marks]

4. Using the table, state what conclusions you could draw from the cost –benefit analysis. [5 marks]

5. You are asked to plan an investigation to estimate the external costs and benefits of the relocation shown in the table. Explain how you might do this and comment upon some of the problems you might foresee. [10 marks]

Chapter Eight

Environmental improvement in theory: private action

'How, from shelves stacked with products labelled "non-toxic", "recycled" and "natural", does the consumer know which to take seriously?'

This chapter looks at the highly pro-market view – *that private action, not involving the government, can solve environmental problems.*

Coase bargaining, private property and mergers

We saw in Chapter 3, with the example of the over-exploitation of fishing fields (Figure 7), how externalities can arise with a common property resource, owned by nobody and to which everyone has free access. As the economist Coase has pointed out, common property resources are likely to be misused and wasted. For instance, it is said that the reason the Indian elephant survives is because it is privately owned, whereas the African elephant, an endangered species threatened by poachers – even in game reserves – is common property.

The Coase argument (point 3 in the boxed summary) appears to stand on its head the conventional wisdom that the polluter pays. However, the polluter is not always rich and powerful and the pollutee is not always poor and helpless. If polluters are countries that are less well developed, or with inadequate technology and resources, then financial inducements from the 'victim' are essential. Examples of the victim paying the polluter can be seen in the case of technical aid from Sweden to help Poland reduce its emissions of sulphur and nitrogen oxide that cause acid rain, and a greements to transfer technology to China and India to assist with curbing CFC emissions.

Why, according to Coase, is the efficient outcome not affected by who owns property? Imagine a factory whose operations require discharge of some waste into a river, which is also used by a firm running a holiday camp with recreational bathing, boating and fishing. Suppose an efficient solution requires the factory to install filtering equipment to remove unsightly and toxic substances from the effluent,

---

THE COASE THEOREM SUMMARIZED

1. If property ownership is well defined, individuals well informed and bargaining costs not high, then the parties involved can bargain to their mutual benefit.

2. Externalities, positive or negative, will be internalized and included in the negotiated price, allowing a socially efficient output to be achieved.

3. Irrespective of who owns the property rights, a socially efficient outcome can be accomplished even if the pollutee pays the polluter not to pollute.

4. If bargaining is too expensive, it may be possible to seek compensation for pollution damage through the courts

---

making the river safer and more appealing to holiday-makers. The impact of the filtering plant on the factory and the holiday firm is shown in the first two columns of Table 8.

If the factory owned the river with the right to discharge waste, the holiday camp would gain if it paid the factory to install a filter. It might, for example, be prepared to pay up to £300 000 – half of its anticipated increase in the profit with a cleaner river – which more than compensates the factory for its fall in profits using the filter. Alternatively, if the holiday camp owned the river, with a right to clean water, then the factory would be compelled to install a filter if it wished to discharge waste. Regardless of property ownership, the same efficient outcome is achieved – filtered river water. The only difference that ownership makes is in the distribution of profits.

A merger of the two firms also solves the problem. Because the increase in total combined profit (the last column in the table) accrues

Table 8 Factory/amenity example

	Factory profits (£)	Holiday camp profits (£)	Merger (£)
No filtering equipment	900	200	1100
Filtering equipment	700	800	1500

FRUIT AND HONEY

Fruit-growing and bee-keeping provide a good example of how Coase bargaining deals with, in this instance, positive externalities. Bees are essential to pollinate fruit blossom, which in turn provides the bees with nectar for honey. The positive externalities arise because extra fruit trees bring extra benefits to bee-keepers for which they do not have to pay. Also, extra beehives bring free benefits to fruit-growers. Theoretically we might expect an under-supply of orchards and bee-hives. However, because property rights in both are well defined, orchard-owners with trees low in nectar yield will pay bee-keepers to place hives in their orchards to achieve effective pollination. Conversely, bee-keepers will pay orchard-owners where there is high nectar-yielding blossom needed for honey.

to the merged company, there is a powerful incentive to install filtering plant. In this case, the diversification by merger internalizes the externality. The firm Ready Mixed Concrete, for example, diversified in this way into the leisure industry. The unsightly water-filled craters – an externality – left by its gravel digging were attractively landscaped and turned into a marina and theme park. However, mergers are usually undertaken to secure economies of scale and finance. They do not offer a general solution for externalities.

Implications and objections

For market enthusiasts, the Coase analysis appears to convey strong pro-market messages:

- If individual property rights are well defined, government action will not be needed. Private bargaining will deal with externalities.
- If common property resources are privatized and run for profit, by charging users for access, then most environmental problems would be solved.

We can identify several objections to the analysis.

1. Inefficient bargaining

Bargaining over externalities may be prohibitively difficult and expensive because thousands of polluters and pollutees are involved. With so many interested parties, free-riders are almost inevitable. Each individual has an incentive to leave others to do the work, but hopes to reap the benefit. Consequently insufficient effort goes into the bargaining. Frequently information for efficient bargaining is lacking. This is a problem of **asymmetric information** – buyers and sellers have different information about a transaction. The exact sources of pollution may not be known. Moreover, one party may incorrectly believe that it can secure big advantages by tough bargaining. The factory in the example above might demand £600 000 and the negotiations would fail entirely.

In the real world, the ownership of property has a strong impact on bargaining outcomes. Farmers, for example, are a powerful and persuasive political lobby, influencing government legislation within which negotiations about externalities occur.

2. Privatization and externalities
Private ownership of property is clearly irrelevant in the case of a major source of externality – air pollution. It is also unlikely to deal adequately with over-fishing and ocean pollution. Quite apart from the trouble of satisfactorily dividing the world's oceans between countries and transferring ownership to private corporations, there remains the difficulty that fish will swim freely between seas; similarly with the movement of current-borne pollutants. Private ownership alone does not ensure the detection and policing, on an international scale, of the dumping and spillage of pollutants.

The failure of private ownership to deal with externalities arising from cross-boundary problems is also seen in agriculture. Toxic fertilizers used on one farm can percolate through the soil to underground aquifers, contaminating water supplies over a wide area. Likewise, new breeds of pesticide-resistant insects will move freely between farms.

Unless all externalities are internalized and appear in a firm's balance sheet, private ownership of resources provides an incomplete answer. Privatization of forests, for example, might save timber but will not save a single species of plant or animal if such preservation is not profitable. Even reforestation cannot be guaranteed if a logging company has a large enough acreage of timber to last over what it sees as its foreseeable lifetime.

The preservation of endangered species (see the boxed item) is a further example of how property rights do not get all relevant values on to a balance sheet and included in decisions on the best use of resources. Rhino and elephant farms may succeed in saving the animals, but is this the preferred solution? The 'for profit' answer is regarded by some as a distasteful variant of factory farming. Many people place a higher value on protection of wildlife in its *natural habitat*.

Altruism

If people are sufficiently unselfish (altruistic) and well informed, then in deciding between two almost identical products A and B they will buy B, the more expensive but less environmentally damaging product. In choosing B, consumers are internalizing the externality that exists with A. If there are enough buyers, profitable markets for green products will develop and many environmental problems will be solved.

Increasingly consumers have opportunities to buy environment-friendly products which sell at a premium. For example, they have a choice between free-range and battery eggs. There is no longer just 'timber' – there is wood from sustainable managed forests and wood of dubious origin (sometimes extracted illegally from indigenous native and biological reserves). There is even the possibility of buying green electricity generated from renewable sources like wind, water and methane gas from rubbish. For such electricity customers would be

Rhino and elephant farms 'would save species'

DAVID NICHOLSON LORD

BIG animals such as rhinoceroses and elephants should be 'privatized' to save them from extinction, according to a leading South African wildlife researcher.

Rhinos, for example, should be farmed for their horn, which is widely prized for its medicinal and aesthetic properties and can be harvested without killing the animal.

International measures to curb trade in endangered species and conserve dwindling numbers appear to have failed, Michael Sas-Rolfes told a conference in London yesterday. Both elephant and rhino poaching continued despite millions of pounds spent by government and voluntary bodies.

Mr Sas-Rolfes is preparing a report on the rhino-horn trade for Traffic, a British-based body monitoring trade in endangered species and funded by the World Wide Fund for Nature and the IUCN (World Conservation Union).

He told the conference, organized by the right-wing Institute of Economic Affairs and described as the first in the United Kingdom to propose free-market solutions to environmental problems, that the 'mental block' of Westerners about the commercialization of wild animals could propel many species into extinction.

He argued that the international ban on ivory has only affected Western countries, and demand for rhino horn remained 'substantial' and was unlikely to be reduced. 'As long as there is some demand, rhinos will continue to be under pressure,' he said.

The Independent, 17 April 1994

expected to pay a premium price – possibly 10 per cent more than ordinary bills.

Assuming shoppers can afford green products, there remains the problem of asymmetric information. Buyers are often less well informed than sellers about the qualities of the products they are buying but also less able to interpret conflicting claims made about them by experts. Witness the controversy over genetically modified (GM) foods. Despite the claim that 25 000 field trials in 45 different countries, involving 60 different species, demonstrate the safety of GM foods, consumers are unconvinced. Fears remain about possible long-term effects on health and the environment. The public need to be reassured not only about

From poachers to gamekeepers

The timber industry is turning over a new leaf. These days, environmentalists are not the only people who are proclaiming the importance of protecting trees. From forestry companies to superstores, those who make their livings cutting them down and selling the resulting wood are also interested in being seen as green and wholesome. And what better way to achieve that image than a certificate issued by a respectable conservation group?

The most respectable of all the groups that certify the ecological soundness of the management of forests is the Forest Stewardship Council (FSC), which is based in Mexico and backed by the World Wide Fund for Nature (more familiarly known as WWF). It was founded five years ago by a coalition of conservation organizations, indigenous people's groups, forest managers and timber companies, and it now has 257 member organizations.

The FSC aims to give wood-buyers a guarantee that their supplies are not harming local people, exploiting their workers, killing rare animals or raping virgin forests in the search for profitable timber.

Although other national and industry schemes also guarantee timber's green credentials, the FSC has the advantage of global standards for accreditation. In Britain, for example, the '95-plus' group of environmentally concerned companies includes firms such as B&Q (a hardware chain), Asda (a supermarket) and Ellis Hill (a timber importer), who want a simple, universal standard to show that their products can be bought with a clear conscience. The FSC provides them with one.

But do shoppers care whether their wood is grown in sustainable forests? Few seem prepared to pay a green premium – B&Q's most optimistic estimate suggests that 15 per cent of its customers might. On the other hand, if all else is equal, shoppers do prefer a store with a responsible image. That gives firms an incentive to improve their green credentials, and hope to trade off the extra cost against a higher turnover.

The Economist, August 1998

the quality of GM testing and licensing but also, as an important first step, by clear labelling. This at least gives them the choice of buying non-genetically modified foods. But is labelling the answer to creating a market for green products?

How, from shelves stacked with products labelled 'non-toxic', 'recycled' and 'natural', does the consumer know which to take seriously? Which is greener – a product made of bio-degradable material or of recycled material? Competing claims to greenness may be confusing for consumers and difficult to evaluate (see the boxed item). Many products are virtuously claimed to be 'green' but how many really are? The label 'recyclable' may mean very little when there are inadequate facilities to salvage cans and wrappers. The 'Earth' beer – presented as a breakthrough in environmental products, with the slogan 'Suntory thinking about the Earth' – offered nothing more revolutionary than a stay-on can opener.

In this setting it is easy to see how **Gresham's law** (bad drives out good) will start to operate. First enunciated by Sir Thomas Gresham (Advisor to Queen Elizabeth I) after an enquiry into the debasement of the coinage as 'Bad money drives out Good', this was later adopted as a metaphor for any market situation in which buyers prefer the cheapest goods, mistakenly believing them to be indistinguishable in quality from the more expensive. The consumer may not know if product A (more expensive) is genuinely environment-friendly, but suspect that the claims are simply 'marketing hype'. The good products will be undercut by the bad and it will become increasingly difficult to sell genuinely green commodities. Because of asymmetric information, market forces will not ensure a socially efficient outcome. A case can be made for some kind of regulatory body, assessing and validating the claims of eco-labels (see Chapter 9). *The Economist's* article 'From poachers to gamekeepers' well illustrates the importance for consumer confidence of a labelling authority that is seen to be independent.

Summing up

- Economic analysis shows that government action to deal with environmental problems will usually be more successful if it harnesses market forces, instead of replacing them entirely by direct regulation (CAC). Nevertheless, for practical and political reasons, CAC systems remain widespread.
- Private action based on property rights (Coase bargaining) or altruism will generate, through market prices, strong but inadequate incentives for the best use of environmental resources.

- Market forces alone will not solve environmental problems. Government intervention is needed to support and guide private action towards a better environment.

KEY WORDS

Coase theorem   Gresham's law
Asymmetric information

Reading list

Anderton, A., Unit 37 in *Economics*, 2nd edn, Causeway Press, 1995.

Bowers, J., Chapter 4 in *Sustainability and Environmental Economics*, Longman, 1999.

Mankiw, N., Chapter 10 in *Principles of Economics*, Dryden Press, 1997.

Perman, R., Common, M., McGilvray, J. and Ma, Y., Chapters 7 and 8 in *Natural Resources and Environmental Economics*, Longman, 1999.

Useful websites

DETR: www.roads.detr.gov.uk/roadnetwork/heta/hetacoba.htm

Severn–Trent: www.severn-trent.com/

Essay topics

1. A chemical company is known to discharge effluent into the local river.

   (a) Using a diagram, explain why this is indicative of market failure. [10 marks]

   (b) A local environmental group wants to close the chemical company down. An economist suggests using indirect taxation to deal with this problem of perceived market failure. Assess the relative merits of these two policies as a means of improving resource allocation. [15 marks] [OCR board 1996]

2. In July 1996, it was reported that Huddersfield's 330 ft high waste incinerator would be closed in 1997 owing to public pressure on account of dioxin pollution levels facing nearby residents being 187 times higher than the EU safety limit. As a consequence, the local council is faced with the serious problem of how else it can dispose of household waste.

(a) With the aid of a diagram, explain how the incinerator's operations lead to negative externalities for the community. [10 marks]
(b) Evaluate how cost–benefit analysis might be applied to determine how best to dispose of waste that was previously incinerated. [15 marks] [OCR board 1999]

Data response question

This task is based on a question set by the Oxford and Cambridge Schools Examination Board in 1999. Study the information and then answer the questions that follow.

The problem of pollution

Every day, there are innumerable instances where firms and other organizations pollute their local environment, deliberately in the main but sometimes by accident. The extract below, taken from the *Daily Telegraph* of 6 August 1996, reports on a particular case whereby the polluter was successfully prosecuted for the environmental problems caused by a spillage of chemicals into a local river.

Water firm fined over salmon deaths

A water company was fined £175 000 yesterday for poisoning a salmon river. Severn Trent Water admitted leaking chemicals into the Wye, killing 33 000 young salmon – 98 per cent of the stock in the river.

Cardiff Crown Court heard that the leak was the company's thirty-fourth conviction since privatization in 1990. Judge John Prosser criticized the company for its poor record and described its management as 'very slack indeed'. Mark Bailey, prosecuting for the National Rivers Authority, said that pollution from the Elan Valley water treatment works, at Rhayader, Powys, had 'catastrophic consequences for the river'.

'An estimated 33 000 young salmon were exterminated by this leak, which affected eight kilometres of river,' he said. 'It is relatively easy to replace adult salmon, but these young salmon need to be replaced with the fish from the same gene pool. Severn Trent caused this catastrophe through a collection of errors, including bad management and inferior maintenance. The area is one of the most significant salmon fishing areas in England and Wales and this is one of the most significant incidents. The sheer number of fish killed is higher than any other incident.'

Judge Prosser told water company executives sitting in the court that the leak was due to design defects, gross mismanagement and inferior maintenance. The company also claimed it was not responsible for the whole of the pollution.

Incidents such as the one described are the outcome of a situation whereby the market mechanism has failed to produce the best allocation of resources to negative externalities. Economists can explain the pollution of the River Wye by Severn Trent Water in terms of a diagram like the one reproduced here.

Private and social cost divergence

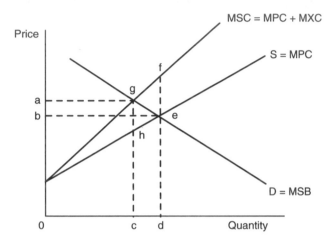

(MXC = marginal external costs; MPC = marginal private costs; MSC = marginal social costs; MSB = marginal social benefit)

1. (a) Explain what is meant by a negative externality. [2 marks]
   (b) Use the evidence in the newspaper article to show how negative externalities apply to this particular pollution incident. [6 marks]
2. Use the figure to answer the following questions and, in each case, assume a competitive market operates with no government intervention.
   (a) What would be the market equilibrium price and output? Explain your answer. [4 marks]
   (b) What would be the price and output at the social optimum? Explain your answer. [4 marks]
   (c) What are the consequences of the differences between price and output levels at the market equilibrium and the social optimum? [6 marks]
3. (a) Drawing upon the case described in the newspaper article, explain the arguments for and against fines as a means of reducing environmental pollution. [6 marks]
   (b) With the help of the figure, explain how a pollution charge or

green tax might be applied in theory. [6 marks]

(c) Discuss how effective such a charge or tax might be in this particular case. [6 marks]

4. Suppose the National Rivers Authority takes action to close the present Elan Valley water treatment works and recommends its replacement with a new works in a different site. Discuss how an economist might investigate the case in favour of closing the present water treatment works and choosing a new site. [10 marks]

Chapter Nine
Environmental improvement in practice

'The regulatory approach has served Britain and other countries well in the past and will continue to be the foundation of pollution control.'
This *Common Inheritance* – first report, September 1990

'Economic instruments are inherently more flexible and cost-effective ways of achieving environmental goals. The government believes that the time has now come to deploy them more fully.'
This *Common Inheritance* – second report, October 1992

Inevitably, because of our membership of the European Union, much of the environmental legislation now affecting the UK originated in Brussels. However, there are some British initiatives worth noting.

The quotations heading this chapter are taken from an important government statement, *This Common Inheritance*. The **regulatory approach** and the use of economic instruments are entirely different – and some would say opposite – ways of dealing with environmental problems. In Chapter 7 they have been described as CAC (command and control) and EI (economic incentive) systems. In practice, the government uses a combination of the two systems in the following ways.

Integrated pollution control
The core of UK policy is contained in the **Environmental Protection Act 1990**, a key element of which was the establishment of **integrated pollution control (IPC)**. IPC recognizes that all the various elements in the environment are inextricably linked. By considering the total impact of releases to the air, water and land, the aim is to ensure that no one element is protected at the expense of others.

Regulation
Implementation of integrated pollution control in the UK is the responsibility of the two authorities established in 1996: the Scottish Environment Protection Agency and, for England and Wales, the Environment Agency (EA). The latter was formed from a merger of its separate predecessor bodies – HM Inspectorate of Pollution, the National Rivers Authority and local waste regulation authorities – providing a more streamlined service for the delivery of efficient IPC.

Pollution watchdog has bark worse than his bite

Last year the biggest fine the Government's £500m-a-year Environment Agency won from prosecution was £175 000. In the dock was Severn Trent Water, the second largest water utility, which killed 33 000 fish in a river in mid-Wales – its forty-second pollution offence since privatization in 1989.

It was 'the equivalent of a £15 fine on someone earning £30 000 a year', Ed Gallagher, the agency's chief executive, said yesterday. He told the organization's first annual meeting that big companies can shrug off the little fines they receive for major pollution offences. 'These fines are really small change to these companies – they send the wrong signal to the boardroom and the public.'

Magistrate courts can impose a maximum for a pollution offence of £6000, while in the Crown Court there is no limit. The agency does not want these maxima changed; it just wishes magistrates and judges would use their discretion to push the level of fines upwards.

The more consented, legally authorized pollution a company produces the more it should pay, argued Mr Gallagher. And if it breaches its consent it should also have to pay extra, even if it was not taken to court and prosecuted. 'The polluter pays principle is one of the few things everyone can agree on,' he said.

Friends of the Earth protesters demonstrated outside the meeting, claiming the agency had too cosy a relationship with industry and did not prosecute companies which breached their consents often enough. But the pressure group welcomed the call for stiffer fines.

The Independent, 17 September 1997

All firms with processes likely to pollute must first obtain authorization from the EA, which can set specific conditions that operators must meet – for example, requiring them to minimize emissions or to make emissions harmless. An authorization is supposed to be granted only if the firm deals with pollution using the *best available techniques not entailing excessive cost* (BATNEEC). A record of all applications from firms and organizations is available for public scrutiny.

Under the Environmental Protection Act, directors and managers can be personally liable for their company's pollution. In theory, although so far never in practice, criminal charges can be brought against them and they can be sent to jail. The EA is considered to be the most vigorous pollution control body in Europe. On the face of it, the UK appears to have a tough but fair regulatory (or CAC) regime. Nevertheless, there are doubts about its efficiency and effectiveness. Specifically:

- the system is prone to regulatory capture (see Chapter 7)
- the level of fines and fees, despite recent increases, is not yet high enough to have any significant impact on corporate offenders. In 1998 the average fine for prosecution was only £2786
- more extensive use needs to be made of cost–benefit analysis to ensure that, as the economist Dieter Helm has claimed, the 'BAT' element of BATNEEC rule is not applied more than the 'NEEC' part.

Economic instruments

The problems with CAC systems are acknowledged by the government. The publication of the second report *This Common Inheritance* in 1992 restored the principle of economic incentives to centre stage, with the statement that in future '*there will be a general presumption in favour of economic instruments*'. This was further underlined in the 1994 version of *This Common Inheritance*, which emphasized the government's commitment to deregulation in favour of market forces:

> '...there is always a risk that regulation will impose unnecessary costs on industry.'

The report summarized the advantages of economic incentives and gave examples of the government's use of them (see the boxed item). The following three sections review the application of economic instruments in the UK to water, roads and waste disposal.

● Water

To the list of economic incentives should be added the effect of water privatization under the Water Act 1989. This has meant that the cost of investment needed for environmental improvements in cleaning up beaches and river waters is now reflected in water charges which have risen by a controversial 42 per cent above the rate of inflation.

Monitoring by the EA appears to show that people are beginning to get cleaner rivers and beaches, although green pressure groups dispute this.

Prior to privatization, government minsters were often defensive and sometimes evasive about the poor standard of water – but, fearful of unpopularity, they were reluctant to raise prices. Now with no financial responsibility to the water companies, they can be more critical of water standards and charges. A dramatic reversal in MPs' attitudes to water charges was seen in 1998, when the cross-party House of Commons Environment Committee attacked the policy of the water industry regulator – the Office of Water Supplies (OFWAT) – for

ECONOMIC INSTRUMENTS

Extracts from *This Common Inheritance*
Third report, 1994 (Cm 2597)

Economic instruments work by putting a price on the use of the environment and include emission charges, product charges and tradeable permits. They have several major advantages when compared with direct regulation:

- cost-effectiveness
- innovation
- flexibility
- informational efficiency
- public revenues.

Existing instruments or fiscal measures which have environmental effects include:

- the tax differential between leaded and unleaded petrol, which has been very successful in stimulating sales of the latter
- recycling credits to reflect the saving in disposal costs which result from recycling domestic waste
- VAT on domestic fuel and power, which should encourage energy efficiency in the home and contribute towards achieving the UK's carbon dioxide target
- a commitment to raise fuel duty by at least 5 per cent a year in real terms, which should help to meet the UK's carbon dioxide target
- industrial rationalization arrangements under the Montreal Protocol, to allow firms to trade quotas to reduce the cost of phasing out CFC production.

supporting price cuts in water charges. The MPs wanted no cuts so that more money could be spent on curbing sewage pollution on beaches and rivers – a view that would have been unlikely before privatization. They criticized the regulator and regretted that 'he chose to interpret his duty to customers only as protecting their pockets'.

There are strong incentives for environmental gain but much hinges on the effectiveness of the regulator to ensure that cost increases are fully justified and the burden distributed fairly between consumers and shareholders. We are also dependent on the vigilance of the EA in checking that higher quality water resources are being achieved.

● Traffic

In 1997 the Royal Commission on Environmental Pollution reported that UK transport accounts for the whole of the forecast increase in CO_2 emissions – the main greenhouse gas – between 1970 and 2020. Two-thirds of the rise is generated by private cars, which emit three times their own weight in greenhouse gases every year. Britain's roads rank among the most congested in the European Union. In these circumstances public transport appears to offer distinct benefits: not only does a single bus carry as many passengers as 60 cars – or 1000 cars in the case of a train – but it is energy efficient and environmentally friendly.

The Government's 1998 White Paper on transport policy proposed a number of economic incentive-type measures to persuade car drivers to drive less:

● improving the attractions of public transport – frequency, reliability and information
● encouraging motorists to make more use of public transport by road pricing and other charges
● because a quarter of all trips are local – less than two miles – giving local authorities a leading role in levying new charges for road use and parking and allowing them to keep the revenues raised to spend on approved public transport projects.
● more bicycle paths; safer routes for children to walk to school.

The aims of this policy document have also found some expression in the 1998 and 1999 budgets, with a 6 per cent increase above inflation in fuel duties together with other measures to encourage the use of smaller cars and cleaner fuels.

But as numerous critics have argued, substantial investment in public transport is needed to make it sufficiently reliable and comfortable to even begin to tempt motorists to consider a switch from private cars. It is unlikely that adequate resources will be forthcoming or whether, to judge from the experience of cities like Toronto, such investment always provides a solution. As more people move to the suburbs, it becomes increasingly difficult to devise a public transport system flexible enough to cater for diverse routes to work and leisure destinations.

In principle a comprehensive road pricing scheme and other green transport charges, by signalling the real environmental costs of private motoring, should shift demand towards public transport. In practice politicians, fearful of the wrath of motorists, are understandably timid about such solutions. For example, the majority of the Government's opinion panel is opposed to road pricing.

Road pricing runs into trouble with Blair focus group

John Prescott's flagship road pricing policy has run up against fierce opposition from the Government's own mass focus group.

Nearly 60 per cent of the 5000-strong People's Panel oppose Labour's plans to cut traffic jams and pollution by charging motorists £2 a day to drive through town centres.

The panel, which was set up by Tony Blair last year to make Whitehall more responsive to public opinion, was found to be overwhelmingly against increases in car parking charges and cuts in road building to fund public transport improvements.

The depth of opposition to Mr Prescott's key transport policies was revealed in a wide-ranging Mori survey of the panel's views, published by the Cabinet Office.

However, it was the Secretary of State for the Environment, Transport and the Regions' plans to raise extra funds for public transport that raised most objections, proving that the Government has a long way to go before winning popular backing for the measures.

Contrary to expectations the study found that 60 per cent didn't think that traffic congestion was a problem in their area and 78 per cent didn't believe that air pollution was a concern. More than half of those questioned were against cutting road building, three-quarters opposed car park charge increases and four fifths disliked petrol price hikes.

Cabinet Office officials claimed that the panel was a "world first" which used a representative slice of the population to keep ministers in touch with public opinion.

The Independent, 30 January 1999

● **The waste disposal problem**
As in so many other countries, waste production in the UK has risen significantly with the development of industry and increases in population and consumer spending. The total amount of waste

produced annually in England and Wales is now estimated at over 145 million tonnes.

Although 100 per cent recycling is neither feasible not economically desirable (see page 19) the questions remain: Does the market ensure that the disposal of this waste is efficient? Is an appropriate balance struck between recycling and disposal on rubbish dumps – landfills? Eighty-three per cent of the waste collected by local councils is sent to landfill sites, and 70 per cent of waste from all sources is dumped.

Because of the externalities of waste disposal, markets will give distorted price signals and resources will be inefficiently allocated. This is shown in Figure 12.

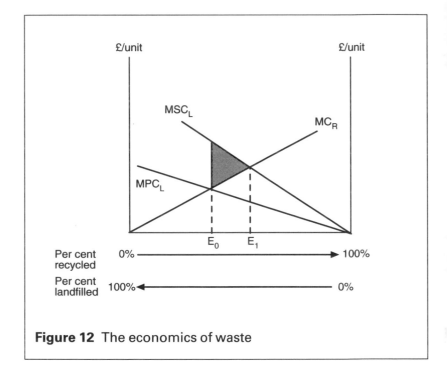

Figure 12 The economics of waste

The position on the extreme left of the diagram represents a situation in which *all* waste is landfilled, while on the extreme right *all* waste is recycled. Moving from left to right, as recycling rises, the marginal cost of recycling (MC_R) increases owing to additional costs, principally transportation over greater distances. Similarly, moving from right to left, as landfill rises, the marginal social costs of landfill (MSC_L) will also rise.

It can be seen from the lower curve that the marginal private cost of landfill (MPC_L) is less than the marginal social cost of landfill (MSC_L). This difference between the two curves arises because dumping in landfills creates external costs not included in the market price for landfill use:

- loss of land for amenity
- the production of leachate which can contaminate ground waters
- the emission of harmful methane gases from decomposing waste
- unsightliness of landfill sites, together with other disturbances such as litter and noise.

The illegal dumping of waste (fly-tipping and other littering) illustrates the problem even more dramatically. Throwing cans and bottles in the street and discarding old vehicles and other rubbish in the countryside may be costless for a single household but the total impact of many households is massively expensive for society.

The MSC_L curve includes all landfill costs. The efficient balance between recycling and landfill is therefore where $MSC_L = MC_R$ (the equi-marginal principle – see page 87) at point E_1, where the total cost to society of waste management is minimized. However, because decisions are based on private costs where $MPC_L = MC_R$, not enough recycling occurs and too much waste at F_0 is dumped. The resulting burden of extra costs on society is shown by the shaded area.

● Some government solutions to the waste issue

In addition to regulations and publicity to educate the public and industry in waste reduction, two economic (market instruments) have been introduced. The aim is to close the gap between the MSC_L and MPC_L curves, so that the externalities are *internalized*. Waste producers will therefore bear the full social cost of their activities, shifting decisions in favour of greater recycling.

A landfill tax

Launched in October 1996, this is a tax on each tonne of rubbish taken to any of the 1700 landfill sites in the UK. Each tonne of waste is taxed at £10, or less for inert waste such as building rubble which is less likely to produce methane gas. The tax is paid by the operators of landfill sites and passed on to the customers. In principle it should work in the manner shown in the emissions tax diagram (Figure 9 on page 85).

Packaging Recovery Notes (PRNs)

Started in 1997, this is an attempt to create a market in pollution permits (see page 90). Businesses with an annual turnover of more than

£5 million and handling more than 50 tonnes of packaging must hold PRNs to prove they are fulfilling their packaging recovery and recycling obligations. Those that recover or recycle more than their required amount can sell their excess PRNs to other businesses recycling less than their required amount. This market should operate as described in Chapter 7 to achieve the target level of recycling at minimum cost.

Although both the above schemes are sound in principle, progress so far has been disappointing. There has been very little trading of PRNs. The administrative problems of running a tradeable permit market, noted in Chapter 7, are relevant here and the scheme is being reviewed by the DETR.

The landfill tax has probably been set too low to have a significant impact despite being raised from £7 to £10 in the 1998 budget. It has also had the perverse effect of encouraging the dumping of waste on unlicensed landfill sites or fly-tipping in country lanes and back streets. A further unintended side effect is that the landfill tax may increase the environmentally undesirable incineration of domestic and commercial waste, since incineration is not included in the scheme.

Clearly further refinements are necessary if it is to be effective.

A mixture of instruments

In the UK, economic instruments are seldom used alone. They are usually supported by a mixture of statutory controls, information, government advice and persuasion. The 50 per cent reduction in airborne lead, for example, achieved since 1983, is due as much to the enforcement of technical standards – cuts in toxic metals in petrol; new cars using lead-free fuel – as to the tax differential of unleaded petrol. A similar comment can be made about the anticipated effect on fuel saving resulting from VAT on domestic fuel and power. The impact of this 'green tax' on fuel consumption will be increased by more stringent energy conservation requirements in building regulations. An Energy Savings Trust has also been established to encourage people to invest in better insulation and energy-efficient boilers. Grants for insulation and draft-proofing are available for low-income households.

It has been claimed that this package of measures will allow Britain to meet its obligations under the Rio treaty on global warming, ensuring that emissions of carbon dioxide are no higher than in 1990. Sceptics claim that the energy tax has more to do with reducing the government's budget deficit than commitments to global environmental problems. They argue that reductions in CO_2 emissions are a bonus. Green taxes certainly enable governments to claim necessities as virtues.

Although environmental taxes may in principle be a more efficient way to raise revenue than conventional taxes, that does not make them popular. This was one of the reasons why the Labour government, in its first budget after it gained power in May 1997, reduced VAT rate on fuel from 8 to 5 per cent. Since domestic and business energy consumption are major sources of CO_2 output, the reduction in VAT rate puts more emphasis on the regulatory approach in reaching the targets to which Britain agreed when it signed the Convention on Climate Change in Rio in 1992 and the Kyoto Protocol of 1997 (see page 48).

● Summary of UK policy

The list of economic instruments in the boxed item on page 109 is a short one. Since 1994 there has been a distinct shift in emphasis towards market based economic incentive schemes rather than command and control (CAC) methods to reach environmental objectives. The Landfill Tax and market in PRNs is just one example. The 1999 budget included 22 new green tax measures – the largest number in a single budget – aimed at moving the burden of taxation to the use of resources that would cut pollution and create employment. Proposed measures ranged from tax breaks for the use of bicycles by commuters to a new energy tax on business to be introduced in 2002, intended to reduce carbon pollution. Nevertheless, the CAC system still predominates for the reasons outlined here in Chapter 7. The following comment in the 1990 version of *This Common Inheritance* remains true today:

'It is as yet rare to find a full market-based approach, in which prices reflect all environmental costs and benefits.'

European Union policy

The European Union must have a role in environmental policy because its member states are neighbours. Since one country's pollution may affect others, co-operation on environmental issues is essential. *But if the producers in the European single market are to compete fairly, the environmental rules under which they operate must, as far as possible, be the same in each country.*

In 1973 the EU's *First Environmental Programme* was launched. Despite this impressive title, Community environmental policy developed in a piecemeal way for the next 13 years. In 1986 the Single European Act (SEA), which removed all remaining barriers to trade, gave fresh impetus to Community policy by consolidating previous environmental legislation. The SEA added a new Article (103R) which expressly recognizes the importance of the environment. This states that action in the Community relating to the environment shall have the following objectives:

- to preserve, protect and improve the quality of the environment
- to contribute towards protecting human health
- to ensure a prudent and rational utilization of natural resources.

The grand policy statements contained in the Article are converted into detailed actions through, among other instruments, **directives,** which under the Treaty of Rome are binding on member states. All directives, including environmental measures, are subject to the principle of **subsidiarity** – so, wherever it is considered more effective, the action necessary to achieve a target specified in a directive is left to each member state.

For example, the *Environmental Impact Assessment Directive,* introduced in 1988, gave force to the principles expressed in Article 103R by integrating ecological considerations into the planning and decision-making processes in all sectors. Under this Directive certain

---

DoT DESIGN MANUAL FOR ROADS AND BRIDGES
Contents of volume II- Environmental assessment

General principles of environmental assessment
- The aims and objectives of environmental assessment and how its results are reported
- The scope of environmental assessment

Mitlgatlon
- Altering the line of the road
- Lowering the road into a cutting
- Screening by planting, earth bunds or barriers
- Moving or creating a natural habitat

Environmental assessment techniques
- Air quality
- Cultural heritage
- Disruption due to construction
- Ecology and nature conservation
- Landscape effects
- Traffic noise and vibration
- Vehicle travellers
- Pedestrian, cylist, equestrian and community effects

---

categories of projects, such as oil refineries, power stations, chemical installations and motorways, must be subjected to an **environmental impact assessment**. An EIA has to identify the effects of virtually every environmental aspect of a project but the way in which the assessment is conducted is up to individual countries. In the UK, for instance, when dealing with motorway projects, the Department of Transport has its own *Design Manual for Roads and Bridges* (see the boxed item). Although this does not guarantee that future roads will be beneficial and beautiful, it does at least force decision-makers to consider environmental issues which they might have otherwise overlooked.

The Community has agreed, since 1973, to over 490 measures to protect the environment, ranging from reducing acid rain pollutants to the conservation of wildlife. Many of these measures are being successfully implemented, while progress on others, such as the Community-wide eco-labelling scheme for environmentally friendly products, is disappointingly slow. If each member state is to be confident that its partners are living up to their obligations under EU law, then effective implementation and enforcement are vital. Free-riding must be discouraged. An EU network of Environment Enforcement Agencies (ECONET) has been established to help develop common approaches to implementation. Established in 1995, the European Environment Agency, which acts on behalf of the Commission (the executive arm of the EU), collects data on the environmental performance of member states and monitors progress against agreed targets.

KEY WORDS

Regulatory approach	Directives
Environmental Protection Act 1990	Subsidiarity
	Environmental impact
Integrated pollution control	assessment

Reading list

Atkinson, B., Livesey, F. and Milward, R. (eds), Chapter 12 in *Applied Economics*, Macmillan, 1998.

Economics and Business Association, Unit 13 in *Core Economics*, Heinemann Educational, 1995.

Hill, B., Chapter 7 in *The European Union*, 3rd edn, Heinemann Educational, 1998.

Munday, S., Chapter 6 in *Current Developments in Economics*, Macmillan, 1996.

Useful websites

European Environment Agency: www.eea.eu.int/
DETR: www.roads.detr.gov.uk/roadsafety/rvs/hen1_9.htm

Essay topics

1. Smoke from chimneys, exhaust fumes from cars and gases from power stations all poison the atmosphere and cause acid rain. The rain then causes forests, fish and wildlife to die and buildings to crumble.

   (a) Use the above comment to explain and illustrate how private and social costs differ. [10 marks]

   (b) Discuss what policies a government might adopt when private and social costs differ. [15 marks] [University of Cambridge Local Examinations Syndicate 1998]

2. As a by-product of manufacturing chemicals, a firm discharges a pollutant into a river which damages a trout fishery. Assess the effectiveness of different policies in bringing about an optimal allocation of resources in this situation. [40 marks] [University of Oxford Delegacy of Local Examinations 1997]

Data response question

This task is based on a question set by the University of London Examinations and Assessment Council in 1995. Read the article, which is taken from *The Economist* of 18 September 1993, and then answer the questions that follow.

Greenery and poverty

When governments announce new taxes, claiming that they will benefit the environment, they tend to be attacked by the environmentalists they had hoped would support them. Green pricing and taxation measures are especially likely to run into a clash between the need for efficiency and the need for fairness. Many environmental resources are clearly underpriced, and therefore over-used. Not only do the prices of goods such as energy and water often fail to capture the environmental costs associated with their production and use; they may be provided for less than the economic cost of their production.

But energy and water (and less obvious examples, such as land use and road space) tend to be provided by the state. Governments often see them as a sort of social service and worry about the way their prices affect income distribution.

A study of several EC [now the EU]countries by Stephen Smith of the Institute of Fiscal Studies (IFS) found predictably enough, that the poor invariably spent a larger share of their incomes on domestic fuel than the rich, while for petrol the opposite was true.

In Britain not only do the poor spend proportionately more than the rich on household energy; they may account for most of the reductions when the price goes up. A study carried out before the imposition of value-added tax at 8 per cent on domestic fuel in Britain estimated that the poor faced the largest increase in taxes as a share of their incomes and would therefore, not surprisingly, cut their spending most. Moreover, as the richest fifth of households use only 30 per cent more fuel than the poorest fifth, the larger percentage cut in consumption by the poor reflects a larger absolute cut. Imposing VAT on domestic fuel may have benefited the environment, but the benefit will have come from those who can least afford it.

The issues raised by energy taxes are echoed in the British debate over water charges. Here, though, the issue is not one of raising a new tax (though the real price of water has risen by over a fifth in the past four years, partly as a result of tougher environmental obligations) but of choosing a new basis for charging. Up to now, water charges have been levied on a rough measure of the value of a customer's home; by the end of the century, Britain's newly privatized water companies must find a different system. Wise environmentalists should want prices to reflect the costs of supply. Trials of water-metering have been carried out by the water companies; they find, in a report published this week, that metering can reduce consumption by up to a fifth.

1. With reference to the first paragraph, explain why 'many environmental resources are clearly underpriced, and therefore over-used'. [4 marks]
2. Using supply and demand analysis, explain and illustrate the effect of value-added tax (VAT) being imposed on domestic fuel. Illustrate your answer with a diagram showing the impact of the tax on consumers and producers. [6 marks]
3. (a) What is the likely impact on income distribution of imposing VAT on domestic fuel? [3 marks]
   (b) Explain one method by which the government can deal with the distributional effects of environmental taxes. [3 marks]
4. Explain why metering of water 'can reduce consumption by up to a fifth'. [4 marks]

Conclusion

'Think Globally; Act Locally.' Bill McKibben, *The End of Nature*

Markets and the environment

This book has shown how many environmental problems are also economic problems because they concern the use of scarce resources. The 'economist' in Ancient Greece – a title derived from the words *oikos* (house) and *nemo* (manage) – was really a steward or estate manager. Not surprisingly, the first texts on economics were really manuals on farming. It could be said that environmental economics takes us back to the origins of the subject – the effective management of natural resources.

If the world's resources are to be used efficiently, information is needed on which assets are comparatively abundant, or scarce, in relation to demand. This knowledge enables us to set priorities for efficient resource utilization – the conservation and sparing use of scarce natural resources; the fuller use of those that are more abundant. In theory this might be achieved by a rigorous system of state planning and control. As the experience of the former Soviet Union and other communist countries has shown, the bureaucracies such command economies create are cumbersome, expensive and inefficient. By contrast, competitive markets rapidly generate information about relative scarcity in the form of prices. At the same time these prices also provide powerful incentives – through income and the inducements of profit and loss – to act on that information and use scarce resources efficiently.

As microeconomic textbooks frequently remind us, the great advantage of competitive markets is that they are – unlike command economies – supposed to achieve this without the need for government regulation and a costly hierarchy of state planning committees. It is the absence of timely information and the lack of incentives to use resources efficiently that has been a fundamental weakness of command economies, contributing to their decline.

Although environmental performance of former communist countries is deplorable, the record of mixed-market economies is also extremely poor, despite the proclaimed virtues of competitive markets. As we explained in Chapter 2, markets appear to produce and deliver private consumer goods quite efficiently, but they often fail with shared public and environmental goods. The American economist J. K. Galbraith described this predicament as one of 'private affluence and public squalor'.

The correct price signals needed to guide producers and consumers in the proper use of environmental resources are either distorted or absent due to:

- externalities
- lack of well-defined property rights
- the environment having the features of public goods – especially the free-rider problem.

The misuse of the environment due to *market failure* is sometimes increased by *government failure*. We expect governments not just to avoid but also to remedy the environmental pitfalls of the market-place. Unfortunately governments frequently fail to take account of the indirect environmental effects of their own policies. In the UK a good example of this is provided by the 1994 report of the Royal Commission on Transport and the Environment, which pointed out that the transport system was

> '... not sustainable, because it imposes environmental costs which are so great as to compromise the choices and the freedom of future genera-tions.'

This comment, it will be noted, raises the issues of *sustainable growth* and *inter-generational equity* discussed in this book. By the year 2025 the projected increase in UK road traffic, on the basis of current policies, is expected to be between 86 and 145 per cent – possibly as high as 300 per cent in some rural areas. This is regarded as unsustainable because of the costs of externalities – pollution, noise and accidents. The inter-generational consequences may follow from irreversible changes in the environment and the loss of alternative public transport.

Among remedies for environmental problems outlined in this book (Chapters 6, 7, 8 and 9) are:

Economic incentives

- improving existing markets with 'green' policies attained by envi-ronmental taxes
- creating new markets – congestion pricing and trade in pollution permits

Regulation

- pollution control enforced by *emissions standards,* or *technology standards* backed by inspection and fines

Green accounting and auditing
- cost–benefit analysis
- national and corporate accounts and audits – showing environmental impacts

The government action needed to deal with environmental problems will be more effective if it harnesses market forces – the first group of options above – *rather than entirely replacing them by direct regulation.* Nevertheless, environmental taxes remain unpopular and the second group of options predominates. An Automobile Association (AA) opinion poll in the UK, for example, showed that 55 per cent of motorists would 'vote against' politicians intending to introduce road pricing or increase other taxes on motoring.

Economics and saving the planet
Does economics provide solutions to the world's environmental threats? Is the economist's toolkit adequate for the task? Undoubtedly its remedies will help, but it must be remembered that important issues which have a great impact on the environment do not arise simply from market or government failure. Examples are the problems created by population growth and the question of who bears the burden of resolving environmental dilemmas.

The latter issue is about equity or fairness rather than efficiency, not solved by market prices. How much of a burden should be borne by current generations for the benefit of future generations? The question of 'who pays?' also arises in the debate over the conservation of tropical rain forests. Developing countries argue, quite understandably, that they should not be expected to forfeit the gains from the economic development of their natural resources simply for the benefit of richer nations.

How highly do we value the environment and how much of our resources are we prepared to put aside to preserve and develop it? The appealing slogan at the start of this chapter is too simplistic. Global action is just as important as putting bottles in the bottlebank. The latter does not necessarily lead to the former. Nevertheless, McKibben is right in stressing the importance of attitudes and our commitment to environmental conservation. It is not the task of economics to solve problems associated with values and attitudes. However, it can help by contributing to a realistic debate about the alternatives that confront us in the management of natural resources and the future of our environment.